Creating Islands of Excellence

Arts Education as a Partner in School Reform

Carol Fineberg

[signature]

HEINEMANN
Portsmouth, NH

To Charles E. Wilson, inspiring educator, charismatic guru to so many, and my dear and mostly patient husband.

Heinemann
A division of Reed Elsevier Inc.
361 Hanover Street
Portsmouth, NH 03801–3912
www.heinemann.com

Offices and agents throughout the world

Library of Congress Cataloging-in-Publication Data

Fineberg, Carol.
  Creating islands of excellence : arts education as a partner in school reform / by Carol Fineberg.
    p. cm.
  Includes bibliographical references and index.
  ISBN 0-325-00603-2 (alk. paper)
  1. Arts—Study and teaching—United States. I. Title.
  NX303.A1F55 2004
  707'.1'073—dc22   2004010030

Editor: Lisa A. Barnett
Production Service: Argosy Publishing
Production Coordinator: Sonja S. Chapman
Cover Design: Night & Day Design
Compositor: Argosy
Manufacturing: Steve Bernier

Printed in the United States of America on acid-free paper
08 07 06 05 04   PAH   1 2 3 4 5

Contents

Foreword

The neighborhood in East Harlem, marked by graffiti and car hulks, was unquestionably distressed. How much, I wondered, could reasonably be expected from the Manhattan East School we were about to visit? It took barely 15 minutes for skepticism to turn into excitement.

Our hosts took us to the roof of the school, where, amid tools, scraps, and the smell of fresh sawdust, seventh graders were assembling the ribs and keel of a 30-foot boat. Not just any boat, but the replica of just the kind of dinghy used on Spanish galleons. Why? Because the students were learning about the Spanish Armada. Their teacher and a visiting artist from Dreamyard, a New York arts in education program, wanted them to create their own sixteenth-century experience.

Young adolescents, presumably indifferent to school, worked with restless laughter. They not only read about Spain and sailing ships. They not only made the dinghy. They figured out how to lower it three stories to the street, how to pay for a rental truck to get it to the Central Park, and then how to sail it in the Boat Pond. It was a dramatic lesson in just how much arts in education can invigorate and even inspire students to learn, think, and accomplish.

It's a lesson that Carol Fineberg keeps teaching us at The New York Times Company Foundation, which she serves as a consultant and with which she created the memorable School

Arts Rescue Initiative, within days of the 9/11 disaster. There is probably no one in America who knows better how to bring the arts to education, for the sake of the arts and for the sake of enriching the entire school experience for all children. She has had a lifetime of experience in the subject from every imaginable direction—as a teacher, scholar, evaluator, public official, and funder. In this book, she offers a distillation of wisdom and enthusiasm that parents, teachers, and school officials everywhere can welcome with pleasure and gratitude.

Her career parallels the emergence of arts in education as a sophisticated, if often misunderstood, field. In these pages, she corrects the misconceptions and shows how to turn the arts into a powerful partner of traditional instruction. Consider, for instance, her reflections in Chapter 4, "Artists in Education," on how as a young teacher she taught Caribbean geography—and how she would love to re-teach it today. She would use videotapes of musical and dance performances, audio tapes of regional music, maps downloaded from the Web, readings from fine Caribbean writers, classes in the African diaspora, and then a live performance of Ballet Hispanico or Viva Flamenco. She makes me wish she were teaching the subject to me.

Her book is full of scenes and insights like that: the Museum of Modern Art learning to excite grade school students, a school in Queens getting every student to do a self-portrait, kindergartners learning not simply how to make a teepee but also how an entire Native-American village was organized.

It is nevertheless important not to hype or misstate the importance of arts education. There are times, she observes, "when the arts . . . contribute" to general academic achievement. But at other times, they do not. "Then what? Do we dump them as being superfluous to the national plans for education? Of course not. Our children need the arts just as much as they need the humanities and sciences."

With this book, the work of a lifetime, Carol Fineberg tells us all how to do it, with a passion for excellence, with a sense of humor, and with art.

Jack Rosenthal

Acknowledgments

Creating *Islands of Excellence* grew out of extensive conversations with my excellent clients who became close friends and fellow soldiers in our battle to counteract the forces of mediocrity that threaten best practitioners in and out of education. I would like to thank Dr. Eva Pataki, retired principal Irving Hamilton, and the District 29 "Annenbergers"; Deb Halpern and the PS 203 Annenberg grantees; Sydell Kane and Lois Olshan from PS 144; Nasha Schmitt and the Alvin Ailey Dance Theater Foundation for their support of Ailey Camps; Jo Irvine and Tina Ramirez from Ballet Hispanico; Sharon Story and the folks at Atlanta Ballet; the pioneers from the Greater Kansas City Community Foundation and the original Kansas City Arts Partners; and Tony Randall and the National Actors Theatre, all practitioners of best practices. Thanks to Alexander Julian, president of his eponymous foundation, and Jack Rosenthal, President of the New York Times Company Foundation, who encouraged me to use their foundations to support new ideas in the field, and to all the School Arts Rescue Initiative grantees and the American Group Psychotherapy Association for providing the grassroots experiences that led to the writing of this book. Thanks to Janet Eilber of the Dana Foundation and Anne Fritz and David Barg, whose innovative thinking inspired many of the ideas in this book. Thanks to Linda Kelly, Gerald Kirshenbaum, and Mildred

Brown, my friends with whom I worked in New Rochelle, where we built a comprehensive arts in education district and proved that it made better thinkers of us all. Thanks to Carol Sterling, Judith York, and Helen Stambler, whose administration of Arts Partners in New York City grappled with the key issues of school reform through the arts. Thanks to the folks at the JDR3rd Fund, the New York Foundation for the Arts and The Learning Cooperative, where I cut my teeth on theories bound to the evolution of arts education practice.

Introduction

For many years I have wanted to write about the positive and negative consequences of combining advocacy for arts education with the various school reform movements. I wanted to share some insights gained through experiences as a student, teacher, school administrator, innovative program developer, teacher trainer, curriculum developer, adviser to foundations, and finally, arts in education evaluator regarding how learning in and through the arts serves as a prism to look at school reform in this country.

As I have begun to assume the privileges accorded me as a senior spokesperson in the dual fields of the arts and education, I am taking great pleasure in speaking my mind, and sometimes discussing issues that some advocates of arts education would rather not air in the open market of opinion. As a grassroots worker in the field of arts education (and arts *in* education, and education pure and simple), I am eager to share how the arts affect general education practices and under what conditions. I have seen dramatic instances where the arts have made a critical contribution to students' learning and behavior. I have seen professional creative artists, either working full time in schools or serving as resident or visiting artists, turn classrooms into working theatres, dance companies, and ateliers for budding painters and sculptors. I have seen students handle video cameras like professionals as they create documentaries about issues of the moment. I have heard choruses so magnificent that I still get goose bumps when I recall hearing them. And I have witnessed with great disappointment exercises in futility where the opportunity to do good art with great educational outcome is lost for lack of supportive conditions. I have seen instructors (artists or teachers or both) who are ill prepared in both the arts and teaching methods struggle to deliver impossible results under the worst circumstances. And I think I know why the good, the bad, and the indifferent seem to flourish in American public education. That is what this book is about.

Oddly enough, as I wend my way through the sixties (the age, not the era), I find myself busier than ever, responding to more and more requests for help from fledgling as well as veteran arts organizations, from school districts and individual schools, and from foundations that want to help strengthen the place of the arts in the lives of children and youth. It seems to me that there is more national and local attention being given to the arts than I can remember. Why so much action in a field that is plaintive in its concern that the arts are on an endangered species list in public education circles?

Partly, I suspect, the answer lies in the fact that arts education advocates have done a fantastic job of telling the American public about the utility of arts education as a pathway to academic success. Partly it is because over the more than thirty years of work by the National Endowment for the Arts, state arts councils, regional and community theatres, local and national music ensembles, museums and galleries, dance companies, and arts organizations that dispatch professional artists to schools, many citizens have grown up with some arts in their schools and want today's children to have more. Partly it is because of the greater emphasis in the field on sequential instruction in art and music, dance and drama provided by credentialed teachers of those subjects assigned full time to schools all over the country. Partly it is because those in the arts look to the elementary, middle, and high schools as a future audience for their work, and they realize how important it is to reach out to students early in the game of education and be with them through their journey through school. And partly it is because many leaders in education see that without the arts our children and youth are deprived of a full and complete education.

It has taken a few decades to face some realities regarding the arts and school reform, however, although warning signs began to appear early in the practice. We began to see both the benefits and limitations of arts programming associated with improvement of schools when we looked at curricula in the arts and the infusion of arts-related practices into the wider curriculum. Some advocates of school reform latched onto the arts as a more enjoyable way for students and teachers to work on skills associated with language and literacy, mathematics and science, as well as technology. Much has been expected of these arts-linked efforts. Prodded by funders of initiatives in arts education, some few researchers in the field are making great efforts to analyze how instruction both in and through the arts can lead to an improved educational climate if not a comprehensive, successful school transformation. It is time that the story of the arts and education is updated.

As I look back on my own education, I am struck by the fact that my life's work was very much eased by the richness of my extensive background in the arts. It may seem obvious, but—especially in the elementary schools—there are few teachers who come out of a liberal arts background. Many of them major in education and then seek a master's in education, special education, the pedagogy of reading, techniques of supervision, or the preparation of curriculum handbooks. With obvious exceptions, today's teachers are not mandated to explore philosophy, delve deeply into literature (global and American), acquire fluency in a foreign language, study the biological and physical sciences, or complete the dreaded mathematics curriculum. This educational paucity was and is less true of secondary school teachers who must have a major other than education in order to obtain their teaching credentials. Elementary teachers, however, are not prepared in large numbers with the requisite background in the arts or, I might add, in many of the subjects outside of their education major. Happily, this situation is being addressed as institutions of higher education are revising curriculum requirements for potential teachers, elementary and secondary.

School districts have developed training and education programs that try to make up for the lack of liberal arts backgrounds of their teachers. Many teachers who were reluctant learners now enjoy the opportunity to master demanding subject matter when they see the practicality of their knowledge, the relevance of philosophy to the lived life, and the importance of figuring out the mathematical consequences of various life decisions.

Writing this book has given me an opportunity to reflect on the education of our young as viewed through the prism of a current effort to make the arts a vital part of the required and elective curricula in this country. I have had the opportunity to observe education close up in elementary and secondary classrooms across the country, and in several other countries as well. I have seen glorious teaching, and I have seen what could only be called educational malpractice.

I have seen teams of teachers and artists take students through a creative problem-solving process that left everyone breathless with excitement. I have seen other teams miss the opportunity to educate by imitating "teacher-proof" recipes designed merely to produce decorative products or superficial stabs at creative processes.

The chapters in this book are organized 1) to provide a kind of educational memoir as a means of understanding the historical background that has connected educational reform and the arts in education advocacy movement, and 2) to discuss the influence of various reform elements as partnerships, curriculum development, methods of instruction, and advances in tracking educational effectiveness, sometimes known as evaluation or assessment. The personal reminiscences are offered in an attempt to highlight how arts education policy making has affected educational practice in real time with real people. And as with all reality shows, the reader will be able to think about how to preserve the best and avoid the worst by seeking the conditions for the former to grow and the latter to disappear.

Personal Past, Lessons Learned 1

As a college graduate of the late 1950s, with a history major, I was aware of huge events and trends in the development of Western culture and technology, and I was particularly well versed in the major influences of post-Colombian American history: the Enlightenment, colonialism, slavery and imperialism, the Western movement, and world wars and their causes—the usual historical canon at mid-twentieth century. I was relatively unaware, however, of what was stirring in American education when I started to teach in an urban junior high school in the 1960s. As a candidate for a Master's degree in secondary education "social studies," I viewed courses in The History of Education with disdain and of no real import in my professional life. Now some forty-three years later, I find that the history and evolution of education, particularly public education, dominates my thinking. I am dogged by George Santayana's warning, "Those who cannot remember the past are condemned to repeat it," as I explore ideas that offer solutions to the educational doldrums of the early twenty-first century.

As elementary school students in upstate New York some fifty years ago, our life was simple. We bicycled to school, lined up, went to our classroom, and stayed there for the entire day. Once a week Ms. Brady, the art teacher, would come into our class, and once a week we trouped to the gym for a ball-throwing workout with Mr. Houlihan. On Fridays we had a test on what Mrs. Drummond taught us in the four preceding days. Ms. Clancy, who doubled as a second-grade teacher, vigorously led us in rhythm band (with what I suppose were Orff instruments) and led us through the sol feggio books that she took out of the closet once a week for us to practice sight singing.

Ms. Brady was not terribly inspiring. She seemed to spend a lot of time teaching us to draw farm buildings. I remember so well the lesson on how to shade a silo and create the illusion of volume. What a neat trick! For the children who lived on farms—and there were several—this was probably very meaningful in the event they were planning to sketch their family farm compound. For us city dwellers, it was interesting to catch on to some visual tricks, but we were hardly invested in the exercise. I also remember that Ms. Brady vacationed in Guatemala (rumors were that she had a boyfriend there). Each year, she would start the class with a series of drawing lessons of objects that she had brought back from Guatemala for us to see and admire. While Ms. Brady taught us, our regular teacher would take a break.

Most of the time, my best friend and I volunteered to run errands for the school secretary during unessential parts of the day, like art! This was before intercoms were installed in schools, and I can recall traipsing all over John F. Hughes School's huge corridors of learning, stopping to spy on my two sisters in their classes. Twice a week, Miss Lockner would appear at school, and magically, some of us would be summoned for our individual piano lessons! My oldest sister, an advanced piano student, had long since graduated to private lessons at Miss Lockner's home. My middle sister was assigned the viola (by whom I do not know), which she played in our shared bedroom to the dismay of both of us! I took my twenty minutes with Miss L (and in the process finally learned how to tell time), painstakingly progressing through the Thompson books of piano pieces and instructions on fingering. I soon withdrew from the piano sessions; I did not enjoy practicing, and no one (certainly not my mother) was there with either bribe or punishment to encourage my staying power. So ended in-school piano lessons until high school.

Hughes School was typical of its time. It housed classes from kindergarten through eighth grade. Music, art, and gym were taught as separate subjects by specialists from second grade on. The junior high school movement had not taken hold yet in Utica. Music and art were subjects taught by credentialed instructors. Some schools had outstanding music programs with bands and orchestras and glee clubs. Others had a bare-bones music program jerry-rigged together for holiday celebrations.

The real highlight of arts education at Hughes was the vivacious, redheaded Miss Eileen McHugo, the marvelously talented music teacher who led the upper grades in song. Her students performed in various citywide events, and the Hughes choir was the envy of all the other city schools. Miss McHugo taught the older girls and boys and prepared us for concerts on all the high occasions: Christmas, Easter, and Graduation. Alas, the extraordinary Ms. McHugo was sadly rumored to have lost her hearing. She moved to New York City, where we heard that she was going to teach in a school for the deaf. We wept at her departure, knowing even then what a rare opportunity we had had to learn music from such a talented teacher.

When family events forced me to move from Utica to New York City, I met an entirely different kind of educational experience. As a sixth grader in midyear, I was enrolled in PS 9, alleged to be an excellent school on the upper west side of Manhattan even though its name was a number! The classes were tracked according to IQs. The highest class was called, euphemistically, the Opportunity Class. I noticed almost immediately that they had more opportunities than the rest of the students to attend cultural events: opera, museums, and symphonic concerts, as well as trips to the Hayden Planetarium. As a transfer student, whose records were to follow (did they ever arrive, I wonder?), I was placed in 6–1, the class just below the privileged Opportunity Classes. We didn't go on field trips. That experience soured me for life on the stagnant tracking systems based on superficial but permanent judgments about students' abilities.

In the sixth grade, Miss Lenahan taught English, social studies, math, and art. We went to Miss S for science once a week, where we watched from afar as she demonstrated such important scientific concepts as how starch is converted to sugar by dropping something on a slice of potato. The school was older than old! The classrooms were honeycombed behind sliding doors that were opened by monitors on assembly days when girls and boys were required to wear white blouses or shirts and dark skirts or trousers, respectively. No blue jeans allowed! Assemblies seemed to be special events where after much was made of "color guard" a guest speaker from the fire department or the local police precinct would lecture us about safety. Occasionally, we were led in song by Mrs. Malloy, who must have been the music teacher.

Art class at PS 9 was hardly inspiring. The kindly Miss Lenahan would distribute manila paper and tell us to draw a storefront in the neighborhood. I choose a millinery store because the only things in the window were faceless mannequin heads with hats on. Easy to do, or so I thought. I think we had crayons to add a little color to our primitive sketches.

Every Friday was test day. And every Monday, Miss Lenahan would rearrange the seating plan so those with the highest marks were assigned to Row One, and in descending order, the other students were seated. Imagine being consistently assigned to Row Five! The cruelty of the practice, with the top students triumphantly planting themselves in the first five places of Row One, and the middle kids wondering what their worth was, shows how easy it is to make what could be a positive practice (weekly quizzes) into something bad. I feel as if I am describing life during Abe Lincoln's days, but it was a practice that had held for close to one hundred years, and yet in fifteen years it would all be changed.

For the next two years I endured the best that New York City public education had to offer, or so I was supposed to believe. The arts became more specialized, as was everything else in what was called departmentalism. The art teacher, Miss Branch, was very concerned that we learn to master block lettering. So for two years we struggled with measuring boxlike letters for our portfolios and various meaningless poster contests. I cannot recall any lessons that would resonate with any contemporary syllabus for middle school art.

Although it is true that, with the help of a yardstick, I can still create a fairly creditable banner headline, the only real truth that I discovered was that I had no talent! The talented girls (the upper grades at PS 9 were reserved for girls, while the boys were sent off to a nearby coed junior high) got to take "talent class," but I was not included in that group nor did I want to be. All of us had Home Economics, where I learned to make applesauce and sewed my graduation dress. Ugh! I have no memory of any paintings or drawings emerging from Miss Branch's class to decorate the institutional green hallways.

The music program was no solace for this émigré from upstate. Mrs. Malloy, although an amenable person with a sense of humor, was no musician. She banged on the piano during assemblies and played scratchy records for us once a week for music appreciation, but she did not seem to have any interest in nurturing musical or any other kind of performance talents. When the time came to audition for entrance to the High School of Music and Art (M&A), I made the cut to everyone's great surprise at PS 9. I had auditioned as a future voice student, and I don't think any teacher at PS 9 knew that I had a voice! The opportunity to attend M&A forecast the course of my future.

When people talk about the golden age of arts education in New York City's public schools, they are talking about other schools and other times, because I never experienced a joyful arts education at PS

9. Hughes School in Utica was much more sophisticated than anything I encountered in New York. On the other hand, if I had been an
opportunity student, my recollections would have been entirely different. It is so important as one looks at schools to peel away the layers
of propaganda to see where the truths lie and for whom.

Music was my talent and my love. By the time I was eight years
old, I could sing the score of every musical on Broadway. I could har-
monize with my friends as we sang camp songs and the emerging
batch of popular folk songs. I could recognize every tune I had ever
heard.

M&A was my savior! From the very first day of school to graduation, I think I was absent three days. Everything about M&A thrilled
me: the teachers, the courses, the kids. The freedom to explore ideas:
capital punishment, the Korean War, the execution of the Rosenbergs,
the Eisenhower years, and the Iron Curtain. We campaigned for Adlai
Stevenson and advocated for the vote for 18-year-olds. Students of
the 1950s are often dubbed "the silent generation" for their lack of
political consciousness, but M&A was a little island of political activity. Petitions for civil rights and civil liberties were as ubiquitous as fly-
ers for concerts at Carnegie Hall. At dismissal time, we bunched
around the St. Nicholas Terrace doors catching up on the latest peti-
tion campaigns promoted by the American Labor Party or *The Daily
Worker*, the newspaper of the Communist Party. We gathered at a regular spot to sing protest songs with one or more of the superb gui-
tarists in our class. Although I was never a communist, I admired
these militant and fiery-eyed peers for their dedication, even if I dis-
agreed with their assessment of the Soviet Union.

Where did all of these left-leaning "red diaper babies," the children of communists or communist sympathizers, come from? They
were prescient critics of American excess. They thought America
needed to expand its working definitions of peace and justice to
include alternatives to capitalism, and even then they looked for a
solution to the obvious economic and racial inequities. I agreed with
their criticism but rejected their naïve assumptions about the Soviet
Union. This was the period of the red scare, and teachers were vulnerable to accusations of "unamericanism" because of their alleged
sympathies for communist and communist front organizations. Loyalty oaths, which were later deemed unconstitutional, threatened the
economic lives of these hard-working teachers. Several went to jail
for refusing to sign loyalty oaths or because they were members of
"subversive" organizations. Although the Feinberg (no relative to me)
law was declared unconstitutional, some of its victims never recov-
ered from this assault on their integrity. My friends and I were vocal in

our support for our teachers, but it was not until the Feinberg law was revoked that the climate of free speech was restored to classrooms. In the passage of the post-9/11 Homeland Security legislation, one can only hope that we are not about to see a similar hysterical persecution of critics of America or members of groups deemed to be suspect.

In the 1950s, high school social studies sequences usually started with a class in Civics. Students explored all the avenues of policy making in a civil society, and I came out of that class hoping that while we lived in an imperfect society, we were about as good as it gets if we practiced the rules of democracy. The trouble was that everyone did not play by the same rules!

At M&A I discovered, along with my friends, such exotic phenomena as foreign movies and off-off-Broadway plays. (*The Fantasticks* opened while I was in high school and finally closed in 2002.) My friends and I spent our weekly allowances on trips to Greenwich Village to sample the bohemian stuff that cool girls wore: dangling earrings and ballet slippers, chunky abstract designs in silver. Occasionally we lapsed into oxford pastel shirts and pencil-thin straight skirts and cardigan sweaters.

Some of my friends went to the New School of Dance to learn the techniques of Martha Graham, Daniel Nagrin, Anna Socolov, and Sophie Maslow among others. These artists were the spiritual and technical backbone of modern dance at midcentury. Their influence and their legacy are now available to newer generations through The Dance Legacy Project, developed by Carolyn Adams and her sister, Julie Adams Strindberg, and located at Brown University.

M&A proved to be an incubator not only for future artists of national importance like actress and singer Diahann Carroll, composer and orchestrator Jonathan Tunick, folk musician Peter Yarrow, music director David Zinman, and artist Bruce Dorfman, but also the future lawyers, physicians, scientists, teachers, scholars, and homemakers, either recognized or not for their talents, but bound together by their joyful memories of M&A. No one has tallied the number of M&A graduates who attend art exhibitions regularly wherever they live, or who support museums with memberships, or who contribute regularly to the financial support of various arts organizations in their communities, or who participate in community theatre and chorales and chamber orchestras, but I daresay they are there in large numbers. We were a precocious lot and active in pursuing our love of the arts. Some of us joined choruses downtown, others took classes at the Y's or the Arts Students League; some got jobs performing with various Broadway troupes, rushing to rehearsals after school.

During my time in high school, teachers were finding their voice in organized advocacy for better working conditions. For two or three years, teachers refused to oversee extracurricular clubs and teams unless the Board of Education would pay them for their service. One of the consequences of this was to install some after-school activities within the regular curriculum: the school literary magazine and newspaper, rehearsals for evening events, and coaching of some teams. By the time the work stoppage was over, a precedent was set so that many of the so-called extras had become permanent courses and part of the regular curriculum.

My college years were anticlimactic after four years at M&A. Smith College, in retrospect, was a wonderful intellectual nest for me. I went to all of my classes and absorbed a formal, classical liberal arts education. My activist days were replaced by a kind of passive acceptance of what my professors taught. Fortunately, I had professors who were important and respected scholars in their fields. I think I felt cowed by so much intellectual power, and I was not yet ready to question what was taught.

Low self-esteem notwithstanding, whatever I learned at Smith ultimately became applicable as a teacher and teacher trainer, as a writer of proposals and reports, and as an analyst of research findings. I learned those skills at Smith and will be forever grateful to this college that develops strong women for a challenging world. I still call upon what I learned about ancient Greek and Roman history, classics of Greek and Roman literature (in translation), the Renaissance and Reformation, European political and intellectual history, American political and intellectual history, ethics, comparative religion, and research seminars in the Middle East and American studies. I studied art history and attended concerts regularly; I took dance classes (modern) and went to the movies a lot! It wasn't M&A, but it was special in its own right. My cup overflowed.

At Smith I learned to write a paper after an ignominious start. Seems I graduated from high school without understanding how to paragraph! With a little help from the Committee on Assistance in Written English (!), I learned to craft a paper regardless of topic with a certain flow so that when I subsequently accepted assignments to write proposals for grants, I could do them quickly and with the desired results. My proposals, which were really written summaries of good and thorough planning, have brought literally millions of dollars to school districts and arts organizations. My writing skills helped me put together persuasive evaluation reports as long as my thinking was clear and I consistently referred to the collected evidence. Ironically,

I recall finishing my last college paper thinking I would never have to meet a deadline again. Ha!

My social conscience was somewhat exercised during the Hungarian Revolution (we sympathized with the students who were putting their lives on the line in an effort to put an end to Soviet rule over their beleaguered country), but we were hardly moved to put our own lives at the edge of any battlefield. We abided by a particularly heinous "honor system" that not only established that Smith students would not cheat (that was okay), but also mandated Smith students to report violators of either academic or social regulations (that was not). It was the latter requirement that I could not understand then or now. It seemed like institutional tattle-telling, a kind of peer espionage that resulted in student court appearances. At any rate, I received a thorough education in history, political science, literature, and art, and I have been grateful ever since.

After college and a short stint in the publishing business, I was back at school. I was greatly disappointed by the difficult time women in publishing had in finding a rung on the career ladder. Sales jobs were out because they were considered too risky for a woman. Editorial jobs for women were most often reserved for the juvenile division. Things were just beginning to change at some of the bigger houses, but at Grosset & Dunlap, the future looked dim for someone with my meager background and fantasies of accomplishment. So I cast my eyes to teaching, but first I needed the proper credentials. A liberal arts education without pedagogical courses was next to useless if I wanted to teach in a New York City school. I looked at my choices of graduate school where I could attend classes and still keep my day job. (Actually, I do believe in pedagogy as a proper preparation for future teachers, and I also do not believe in taking such courses as an undergraduate. There is too much to learn if one is to have something to teach!)

I enrolled at New York University (NYU), matriculated for a Master's degree with emphasis on social studies and psychology, and began my eighteen-month indoctrination into the science, if not the art, of teaching. I enjoyed myself. I liked my classes. The most important lessons I learned in graduate school were organizational and psychological. Organizational lessons taught me how to prepare teaching scenarios—lesson and unit plans, particularly. In Alice McNiff's class we handed in lesson plans every week and got them back with full critiques. Our unit plans, due at the end of the semester, were twenty-page documents with lesson ideas and resources from which any teacher could teach. Everything I learned in Alice's class I could put into practice immediately and forever. She was well ahead of her time in training us to develop methods to evaluate whether our students had learned what we thought we were teaching.

Julian Aldrich taught methods of teaching geography, and he had some very good ideas regarding the use of the Museum of Natural History, where to find slides to use in the classroom, and how to evoke questions from students rather than just telling the story. John Payne was a wonderful teacher of American institutional history, and when he retired, the School of Education named a special reading room for him.

The best professor was a lightning wit who taught me something about experimental psychology despite my math phobia. John Sullivan was a brilliant psychologist who was just beginning to delve into programmed learning. His classes were like a highbrow course in *Jeopardy!* If these are the answers, what are the questions? How does one lead students through a series of questions so that they discover what you want them to know? Programmed learning was just catching on, but it seemed to me it was more appropriate for learning the rules of grammar and usage than the history of psychological thought.

George Dawson was an excellent coach when it came to my student teaching days. He admitted surprise at our first conference that someone from such a fancy college could work so well with "city kids." George's specialty was economics, and a few years later I was able to introduce him to the editors at Collier Books where I worked briefly. He published the first *Economics Made Easy* as a result of that introduction. The Made Easy series was a precursor to the Dummies books of the 1990s and beyond. There is no such thing as a new idea in publishing.

NYU's School of Education was at its own historic crossroads in 1959–1960. It did not seem connected to any of the rumblings that were going on outside the gates. It was much more as if it was ten years previous than what it would be ten years later. The trend toward activism and partnerships with failing schools had not quite begun. Only a few years later, NYU was in the middle of the social revolution of the 1960s, co-partnering experiments in community control of schools and preparing minority teachers for roles as school administrators. But while I was getting my Master's, NYU was a quiet, pleasant but detached institution.

Although I wanted to teach in a high school, I was assigned to Joan of Arc (JOA) Junior High School (J118, Manhattan) on the upper west side of Manhattan for my student teaching. The school was the first "skyscraper" school in New York; its eight floors dominated the narrow west 93rd Street block as a beacon of learning. The student body was a mixture of youngsters, including some recently arrived from Puerto Rico, who were tanned, smiling, and incredibly polite, but a little short on information about urban living. They lived in crowded converted brownstones on the side streets near the school. There was also a cohort of Irish youngsters; they lived along Columbus and Amsterdam avenues in tenements that were soon to come down to be replaced by middle-income high-rise housing. The school also served a group of Jewish youngsters, many of whose parents were refugees from the Holocaust, who lived in the large apartment houses along West End Avenue, Riverside Drive, and Central Park West. Sprinkled among this picture of diversity were representatives of the African Diaspora: southern blacks, West Indians, and Haitians. Soon to arrive would be a flood of Cubans, escaping Castro's revolution. The Dominicans were also escapees, from Trujillo, and also from poverty. Among the school's honored alumni is Bill Lam Lee, former head of the Office of Civil Rights in the Clinton administration.

Here was a school that, staying within "the neighborhood," gathered together a racially and ethnically diverse population, a rare and wonderful phenomenon in those days. It was quite a multi-cultural stew, and thankfully, an opportunity for a great school to teach intergroup relations on the most practical level. There were many friendships across ethnic lines and very few instances of intergroup hostility. The stereotypes were there, of course, but the staff was required to make a conscious effort to promote harmony among the students and a respect for each other's cultural roots. Individual staff members were cautioned if their treatment of students smacked of racism, and the school was well ahead of its time in dealing with those little sparks that, if not treated, will erupt into major fires. Joan of Arc was often mistaken on my résumé for a religious school; in fact, it was named for the statue of The Maid of Orleans, ensconced on her horse at 93rd Street and Riverside Drive. Why Joan? Why there? A mystery yet to be solved.

My student teaching days were filled with happy discoveries. There was a group of us from NYU and Columbia, and we were put under the wing of Peggy Gellman, one of the wisest and gentlest of great teachers. Peggy helped us make the transition to the other side of the desk in her weekly meetings with us. We learned the mysteries of the roll book, report cards, cut slips, fire drills, and classroom management. I have never seen or heard of another school that fostered regular meetings with its student teachers.

I found that I had a knack for teaching. My bonds with the students were immediate and strong, as were my bonds with my supervising teachers. Jenny Blauvelt was an old-time elementary school teacher who had been transferred to JOA when the city created junior high schools by lopping off the seventh and eighth grades from elementary schools and adding a ninth grade from high schools. She was intelligent without being an intellectual. We filled up her lesson plans book together, and I learned some practical ways to deal with bureaucratic demands. Jenny was good humored and generally liked by her students.

One day, while Jenny was leading the class from the fifth floor to the cafeteria for lunch, insisting as always that the kids stay in line and not talk, a little sixty pound girl snapped, leaped out at Jenny, and dragged the astonished teacher down the stairs by her hair. I was at the end of the line and could not get to Jenny fast enough, but Jack Berbarian, a strong giant of a gym teacher heard the screams and with *two* other men, helped separate the little girl from Jenny. The attack was a total shock to everyone; JOA was not a violent school. Things like this rarely, if ever, happened. Poor Jenny was whisked to the hospital, and after months of convalescence finally returned to school toward the end of the semester. Substitute teachers were hired for her, but in fact, I took over and taught Jenny's morning schedule for the rest of the year. (I had NYU classes in the afternoons.)

What lessons should we learn from this experience? First, you never know when some little something might set someone off, especially in school. Second, all acts of violence are not the result of poor teacher behavior. Some critics would have the public think that, but it is not so. Third, when an act of violence occurs, the perpetrator must be attended to as quickly as the victim. In Jenny's case, the child was removed from school immediately, and I am sorry that I do not remember what happened to her. She was a nice little girl, as far as I knew, and I hope that she was mandated to some treatment center and given a fresh start at another school. In my heart, I seriously doubt that my hopes for her came true. She might have been assigned to a "600" school for youngsters who were in need of more intensive supervision. She might even have been sent to a residential school for disturbed youngsters. She might have been sent to Bellevue Hospital, where they had a special lockup for seriously disturbed children. I just don't know.

In retrospect, the incident plays into the current discussion of what to do about children and adolescents who engage in acts of violence against themselves or others. The statistics regarding violent outbreaks tell us that these kinds of incidents are increasing in number, as is the student population in many schools. Was this in play in Jenny's case? At that time, there was one guidance counselor for eighteen hundred kids. Did this make a difference? Could the child's background or other symptoms of disturbance have been detected if there were fewer than thirty-five kids in a class? Might some early intervention have helped this little girl gain control of her temper before it got the best of her and Jenny?

JOA was a good place for someone like me to teach. It was orderly without being authoritarian. It was fun without being mindless. It was challenging to both teachers and students. I decided to accept the principal's invitation to take a full-time job there and teach Core Curriculum to two ninth-grade classes.

JOA was noted for two famous teachers: the principal, Stella Sweeting, and art teacher, Matthew Feinman. Sweeting was unique in many ways. She was brought to this country from England as a young child by working-class parents. Educated in "normal school," the name for post–high school teacher preparation institutions (later, she earned a doctorate in educational administration), Stella established herself early as a creative and energetic teacher and became one of the great educators ever to head a school in New York City.

Originally a principal in a school in Brooklyn, Sweeting was asked to transfer to Joan of Arc when it was a new and wobbling school, a job she maintained for more than twenty years, during which time she and her husband, a wealthy gentleman and her first fan, became generous philanthropists. Mr. Fogelman was a shadowy figure in our lives, but a most generous supporter of any plan his beloved wife hatched. When money was needed for costumes for a festival or a student-developed play in the auditorium, for field trips to the theatre or museums, for membership in organizations that would then serve the school (the Metropolitan Opera, Metropolitan Museum of Art, National Association of Christians and Jews, etc.), money was available. When Stella retired, she endowed a library in her husband's name at Eugene Lang College of The New School University.

Because of Stella's support, Matthew Feinman was able to run the ideal art studio for junior high kids. His youngsters explored painters and paint, learned art history and criticism as they attempted their own easel paintings. Feinman's classes produced outstanding work, which enhanced the main foyer of the building, announcing to all who entered that art was valued here. But perhaps most impressive to this young teacher, Feinman talked about art in the teachers' room. There was always a group of interested teachers gathered around him as he saucily reviewed a recent exhibition at the Museum of Modern Art or the Metropolitan Museum of Art. He would throw out to the group the most thought-provoking questions that somehow tied art to life to kids and schools. A graduate of Tyler, Feinman was an anomaly in the system. He was an exhibiting artist and a formidable teacher.

To this day, former students maintain contact with him. And he is still making art in his late seventies, exhibiting his work despite macular degeneration that has compromised his vision considerably.

JOA was unusual in that programming centered on the Core Curriculum. English, social studies, and guidance mandates were tied into one two-hour class each day for each of the thirty-some-odd cohorts that formed "homerooms." The teacher needed to be expert in all three subjects, and for a while that worked because teachers from a good liberal arts background formed the bulk of the faculty. As specialists in one of the subjects began to dominate the hiring pool, however, fewer new teachers felt equipped to deal with all three subjects. The preparation required to teach Core was awesome, and only a few felt that the ends justified the means! As the popularity of Core declined, the teachers' union movement was on the rise. With the first union contract, a different kind of teaching schedule was mandated, and Core was sacrificed.

As a Core teacher, I knew nothing of the NEA, NEH, or artists in schools, much less the weird-sounding phrase "arts in education." I knew what good teaching and learning was. I was already known as the "go to" teacher, the one the principal sent new teachers to observe as part of their inservice orientation. I led my department in weekly meetings as a sort of chairperson; I represented the school at citywide meetings where some organization or other wanted input from teachers. I was also for a time a captive of labor as the naive chapter chair of the newly formed United Federation of Teachers. All of these experiences reinforced my decision to teach. I loved what I was doing and I was good at it. Confucius was right: those who love their professions never know a day of work. It was all fun, from the class plays we put on (with Elvira Rodriguez as Daniel Webster and Angel Roman as the Devil in a red cape sewn by his mother for the occasion) to the tests we studied for and conquered. I had what was known as the Spanish Honors Class, composed of youngsters with Spanish surnames, who spoke a fair version of conversational Spanish, but who were now going to get a more classical instruction in Spanish language and literature along with Core and math and science—a valiant experiment, no longer remembered.

I was tapped for union membership and a leadership role very early in my first year as a teacher at JOA. Nina Leichter, a much-admired social studies teacher, was chapter chair, and Alice Marsh, the school's remedial reading teacher, was the union's legislative representative in Albany on her off days. These two women had very important roles in the growing of the United Federation of Teachers, and they did not have a difficult time enlisting me in the effort. The union was in its infancy, and before I knew it, we were involved in a strike for collective bargaining rights with the city. We won and began the hard work of advocating for teachers' rights and improvement of conditions in the school. The union has grown large and powerful in the subsequent years, but I have never wavered in my belief in unionism even when it sometimes takes actions that make me quake with anger.

I was on the picket line for the first strike, and we had almost 100 percent turnout from our faculty. I received a call the next morning from an old beau: he had seen my picture in the centerfold of the *New York Daily News* with a group of JOA picketers and warned me that I was about to ruin my career! The blacklist awaited me and my colleagues! His warning proved to be baseless.

For one year I served as chapter chair, attending union meetings and generally finding my way through a job with few guidelines or boundaries. Although I was proud of the union, and well aware of the excesses and unfair employment practices of the Board of Education, I soon realized that union activism was not for me. Always a supporter, I had other interests to pursue, but I never regretted my tiny role in the advancement of the teacher union movement. What I do regret is the history of blaming the union for every stupid concession that the Board of Education has made over the decades, such as disbanding homerooms as mandatory parts of the organization of middle schools. Homerooms are now put to faculties for voting up or down, tossing vulnerable early adolescents into a lost world of coat-bearing, bookless, wandering middle schoolers bereft of proper guidance and oversight. In one school, where the lack of homerooms was a major contributing factor to the daily chaos and anarchy, the principal and district administration were loath to take on the union and make homerooms mandatory. Here was a serious accident bound to happen. It is no accident, however, that the school is now listed as a failing school.

Although the union contract sacrificed flexible scheduling, it launched a new possibility, especially for the elementary schools, and started the trend toward cluster or prep teachers. In the secondary schools, teachers were traditionally given allotments of time to prepare for their classes. Prep periods were simple to build in because students did not travel from class to class as a group. Their programs were individualized, and schedules were created so that teachers had five or so classes with different groupings of students. This is not so in elementary or middle school, where the dominant mode of organization requires whole classes to travel as a group from one academic class to another. This system requires the class to be "covered" if a teacher needs to leave the room. Elementary school teachers had to sneak off to answer's nature's call, hoping that a neighboring teacher would consent to "watch the kids" while their teacher left the classroom for a few minutes.

With the advent of unionism, elementary teachers got "time off" for preparation of classes and a little time to attend to their own needs. This meant, obviously, that someone had to cover the classes left behind. In many cities, as contractual arrangements were drawn up and approved, relief or cluster teachers or specialists were hired. These teachers would go from class to class, relieving teachers for their breaks. Many of the relief teachers were hired from within the school or district organization but given different responsibilities. For example, if the school's fifth grade teacher had been an art major and wanted to "travel" and teach art once or twice a week to a cluster of classes, she might be assigned to do just that. Or if a teacher who could play the piano and conduct the glee club after school wanted to do this during regular class hours during some teachers' breaks, he could do the same. If the school were large enough to need a corps of relief teachers (keeping in mind that even relief teachers could only cover a finite number of classes per day) then a band of specialists were added to the school roster: art, music, physical education, library, and sometimes drama and dance specialties were created in elementary schools where few had existed before.

Like all solutions born of necessity, the birth of the relief teacher did not necessarily accommodate the educational requirements of instruction. Relief teachers often have to serve more than one building during a week. This means having at least two schools with neither as a home base for lack of space. Sometimes teachers teach in School A in the mornings and School B in the afternoons, wasting good instructional time driving from place to place. Sometimes, the traveling teacher feels disrespected, unimportant, just a cover for colleagues. This contributes to very low morale, understandably. It also makes a joke of efforts to create a sequential and steady curriculum in any of the arts domains. By the time the teacher and students are settled in, the period is half over!

At JOA, I began to feel the real impact of federal funding. Suddenly, we teachers were being asked to write proposals for special projects in teaching reading or math, study skills, reading across the curriculum, and other methods that would help the slower readers to attain better test scores. Teacher training became unexceptional; we were either trainers or trainees as mysterious others found money to pay us for our time. By this time Stella had retired and was replaced by one of her protégées, Edythe J. Gaines, one of the first black junior high principals in New York City. Edythe was a charismatic and adventurous leader, but before too long, she was discovered by Harvard, where she accepted an opportunity to matriculate for an accelerated doctoral degree program. With her degree still fresh, Edythe moved on to a succession of higher positions on the career ladder, leaving in her wake a troubled and inept successor who led JOA down the path to mediocrity and subsequent failure. For a while during Edythe's tenure at JOA I was an assistant principal, but six months after she left I accepted a teaching appointment at M&A, my alma mater. While at M&A, I had the opportunity to create some new and lasting procedures for dealing with the challenges of the 1960s and 1970s.

The 1960s marked the end of the compliant student body. With the arrival of the civil rights movement and the later phases of the Vietnam War, students began to feel they had an urgent role to play in shaping policy through protests. The protests gave birth to various efforts at conflict mediation, and I was one of the first to pilot a new position as Coordinator of Student Affairs (COSA), whose role it was to assist in developing ways to channel students' aggressive political behavior into viable school reforms. We created the first Consultative Council in New York, reasoning that if parents, students, and teachers sat around a table with the principal, some rational resolutions to the inevitable struggles over rules, regulations, and curriculum content could be achieved. Our council became the model for the rest of the city and a string of school system chancellors. We provided guidance to those who would march in protest against the war. The student leaders and I were forever immortalized in a photograph in Jim Bouton's *Ball Four*, where he reminisces about the anti-war demonstration in Central Park. He was one of the featured speakers to thousands of high school students who vacated their schools to show their opposition to U.S. bombing of Cambodia an the whole mess in Southeast Asia.

My stay at M&A was for just six years, enough time to see my incoming freshman class graduate and then some. It prepared me for the new adventure I would take as a program officer of The Learning Cooperative, a short-lived but brilliant strategy to sidestep an awkward and constipating set of communication procedures within the school system and connect thousands of teachers with the innovations that were popping up all over the country thanks to federal funds for pilot programs. I found myself agreeing to leave M&A and assume responsibility for several innovative programs that were designed to elevate educational practices primarily in elementary and the newly hatched middle schools. My work there highlighted a new generation of educational reforms that called for great efforts to train principals as leaders, teachers as team members and collaborationists, and students as disciples of John Dewey exploring the muddy waters of knowledge and self-realization with the help of their teachers.

As new teacher contracts called for more specialists in the elementary grades, a national movement to create "teaching artists" or "artists in residence" was gaining momentum. One of the critical beginnings occurred in New York City, when a group of writers approached the then new National Endowment for the Arts to support their work with public school kids who could not or would not write with any degree of competency, much less flair. The origin of this writers in school project and its descendants is well described in the tenth anniversary publication by the Teachers and Writers Collaborative, *Journal of a Living Experiment* (Lopate, 1979). Distinguished and tyro writers found places for themselves where they could teach kids the way they, as youngsters, would have wanted to be taught: to craft language instead of parsing it; to explore meaning and metaphor based on a desire to say what the kids wanted to say rather than the superimposed topic that their teacher thought was appropriate. (More about the artists in schools program can be found in Chapter 4.)

The Department of Education (originally part of the Department of Health, Education and Welfare) disbursed funds in support of programs that would address special needs such as poverty, minority isolation, and the learning of English as a second language. Other funds were created to support innovations in teaching and learning. Some funds were competitive, requiring proposals and budgets, and volumes of paper. Others were distributed on a per capita basis through state education departments to school districts, but whatever the source and destination, all grants in aid required lots of paperwork. Funds were approved for uses such as hiring ancillary personnel (teachers, curriculum experts, teacher trainers, evaluators of impact) to step into classrooms and add their experience and skill to those of classroom teachers in elementary schools and subject area teachers in middle and high schools.

The passage of the first bill enabling the federal government to support local school districts and even individual schools was a hallmark of the 1960s. The impact of this period is still with us as schools and districts struggle to take advantage of the manna from Washington.

As the money began to flow into schools, ambitious leaders learned how to access not only their share but more. Pilot programs, demonstration projects, validation processes, dissemination of pilots, and replications grants all became the common language of savvy school administrators and grantors. As tax laws changed to encourage contributions by corporate and private foundations, more sources of money for public schools opened up.

The 1960s and early 1970s saw the actual enforcement of *Brown v. Board of Education* (1954) under the Kennedy and Johnson administrations. In the South, black and white youngsters learned to go to school together (although many middle class families, black and white, fled the public schools and have yet to return). Efforts to desegregate were assisted by federal money for innovative programs—magnet schools—that would attract or at least maintain a modicum of diversity and end the noxious period of racial isolation. In the North, where de facto as opposed to de jure segregation in schools was eventually struck down by the Supreme Court, the same desegregation remedies, including redrawing some district lines, were instituted. The next chapter describes more fully the various repercussions of these innovations and how they changed the practice of education for the next forty years.

Formation of Arts Education Policies 2

*T*he development of local and national arts education policies over the past forty years has very much paralleled the development of policy in general education. Thanks to the skillful advocacy work of many arts education organizations and sectors of the American public, the destiny of education has been intertwined with the destiny of arts education and vice versa. This chapter describes some of the building blocks of the current policies not only as an acknowledgment of the work accomplished but also as a lesson to new generations regarding how to use the methods inherent in the democratic process to preserve and protect our cultural legacies.

Policy Needs

In the early 1960s, it was clear that something had to be done to preserve and protect the artistic heritage that belonged fairly to every student in America's public schools. The arts as elements of every child's continuous learning experience were getting short shrift from public schools. New relationships between unions and schools, the ever-present business cycle threats, and a national situation where a major war against poverty was compromised by America's war in Vietnam were cutting off badly needed funds to support an appropriate education for children in art, music, dance, and theatre. Although there were some schools where the arts thrived, there were many more schools where there were no teachers of the arts, no opportunities to experience the pleasure of artistic performances and exhibitions, and no mediators who could help children find their own creative voices.

With the arrival of the 1960s, foundations were cautiously beginning to fund innovations within the big city systems. The Ford Foundation led the field with its nationwide implementation of grants for educational reforms including team teaching, new ways of scheduling the school day, and, most controversial of all, "community control." The Rockefeller funds and foundations (there were several) were interested not only in education but also culture and, most visibly, the arts and arts education. Community foundations were forming that attracted families who were eager to contribute to charities but also eager to get tax advantages by donating to community trusts rather than writing out checks to various needy groups themselves. The first community foundation originated in Chicago, in 1915; the New York Community Trust was started by a group of bankers in 1924. As private and community foundations multiplied and grew their financial stake in various cities, so did their political influence. Sophisticated school districts soon caught on that if they courted foundations, they could place themselves in advantageous positions vis-à-vis their school boards.

Corporate foundations were beginning to grow in influence as the tax laws favored community support grant making. The big corporations led the way: Exxon, Mobil, Texaco, Philip Morris, and AT&T, to mention a few. Corporations were particularly eager to use their community service funds to make the cities in which their employees worked attractive places to live, and therefore they knew that supporting the arts and the schools were top priorities. So influential were the corporate foundations that the American Council for the Arts (precursor to Americans for the Arts) periodically published a listing of information about all the corporations making significant contributions to the arts and arts education. Grant seekers could use the book as a guide to their efforts to continually raise money to meet each year's projected expense budget.

The involvement of the Rockefellers and the New York Community Trust signaled to other foundations that it was okay to get involved with the New York City public schools, which had traditionally operated within the budget negotiated with the city and state.

The JDR3rd Fund Arts Education Program was headed by the politically astute and persuasive Kathryn Bloom, an imposing gray-haired lady whose nervous gestures belied a steely mind and strong judgments. She was hired by Rockefeller to head a program that would in effect put the arts back in arts-starved schools. Bloom had been working for Frank Keppel at the time and had developed the Office of the Arts and Humanities at a time when the role of the federal government in education was expanding into new areas. Her approach was novel: Find ways to connect the arts to what subjects were perceived by school administrators as vital and tie them together through programmatic funding. Make alliances with advocates of general education reforms by showing that the arts help improve learning in the basic skills and were therefore important elements of any basic skills program. And so was born the arts in education (as opposed to arts education), which tied the arts with all kinds of learning possibilities: reading, critical thinking, problem solving, math, science, history, school improvement, multiculturalism, anything that was on the must-do menu of school superintendents, board of education members, principals, and state superintendents of instruction. Bloom built powerful coalitions of selected state education departments willing to advocate for the arts and paraded them through the halls of legislatures, where they made the case for state funding of arts education initiatives in the name of school improvement.

With her able staff, Bloom identified outstanding schools and school districts where exciting examples of learning through the arts were going on. She put a spotlight on these programs by coalescing with those national arts organizations that met annually to advocate for more recognition and support. Using a relatively small program budget, she leveraged her modest dollars to get to the planning and policy tables where strategies regarding federal and state support were hammered out. With small grants to support arts education strategies in University City, Missouri, Bank Street College in New York City, and the Mineola, New York school district, Bloom began to set the stage for a more prominent position for the Fund. She commissioned studies on topics that fleshed out the knowledge and ideas pertaining to schools and the arts. With her new allies, she raised the profile of arts education just as budget cuts were drastically endangering any "frills" during a serious national recession. Her efforts complemented nicely the development of education policy for grant making by the National Endowment for the Arts to support artists to work in educational venues, and ultimately to support arts organizations' teacher training and curriculum development projects.

Large-scale advocacy movements have brought the arts to the public's attention with gusto, from a time when partnerships with public schools were virtually unknown, to the current period where partnerships are becoming the norm. In most of the major cities of the United States, various civic and cultural organizations now send personnel to augment regular staff members in both elementary and secondary schools. Major national and international corporations have forged partnerships to advance career preparation for various business sectors, including the arts (see Chapter 4). Bloom's acumen, documented in JDR3rd Fund publications as well as by Stanley Madeja at the University of Southern Illinois, pointed the way to a whole new approach to supporting the arts, demonstrating her natural talent for politics.

Funders who followed in her footsteps, even though they ignored much of the JDR3rd Fund's rhetoric, refined their strategies accordingly:

1. Discover common causes with influential and established organizations.
2. Initiate collaborations with these organizations that would increase the visibility of the necessity of arts in education programs in public schools.
3. Join with other grant makers to fashion collaborative grants to schools and arts organizations in order to demonstrate the power and attractiveness of arts in education programs.
4. Subsidize efforts to document and evaluate pilot programs.

In all ways, gather the best and the brightest educators, artists, and technical assistants to facilitate steps 1 to 4.

This strategy has had several important and not always positive consequences. On the positive side, alignment with educational reform has put the arts on the grant-making agenda in ways that pure arts advocacy had never accomplished. It encouraged sectors of the public as well as educators to look at the arts as a vehicle for school improvement and to consider funding more than token courses in art, music, dance, and theatre when juggling various educational decisions.

On the negative side, this strategy placed arts teachers in the unenviable position of trying to prove that their work helped their students not only to acquire skills and knowledge in the arts but in other areas as well—areas in which arts educators had no direct role to play. A whole new industry of research has developed as a result of these claims involving arts educators in areas outside of their expertise. Funders continue to this day to demand proof that the arts programs they fund have some positive impact on a host of intellec-

tual, social, and economic circumstances. Among the claims that they hope their grantees will defend with evidence are as follows:
Children will:

- Read better.
- Get along better with each other.
- Improve their attendance at school.
- Improve their behavior in class.
- Display a new sensitivity to social problems.
- Demonstrate a heightened sense of history and geography.
- Understand the principles of physical and natural science.
- Demonstrate control over various mathematics principles.

It is difficult to believe that before 1965, writing proposals for funds to supplement education budgets was a virtually unknown practice. With the arrival of the 1960s, however, federal funds became available and by the 1970s, millions of dollars were appropriated to states and localities on both a per capita allotment (Title One) and competitive basis. Some of this money could be used to develop innovations in instruction and curriculum, and it did not take long for advocates of arts education to see a funding source for dispatching artists into the schools and enabling schools to partake of education programs at museums, theatres, performing arts centers, and the like.

Accessing the money was not easy, and a new freelance service was born: proposal writing. Whether it was for the various competitive funds emerging from the Elementary and Secondary School Act or the National Endowments or for Museum Services, grants began to flow to those schools and districts that promoted themselves and played the political game. Not that they did not deserve the funds, but a pattern of "those that have get, and those that have not get not" became very obvious to those of us working on the local level. The less informed, most harried school principals were in awe of principals who attracted six- and seven-figure grants to support not only major learning through arts education programs but also huge professional development opportunities for their staffs.

Meanwhile, advocates of arts education who were not funders discovered strategies that worked for them which complemented those that Bloom and Keppel had first developed:

1. Organize into one voice for specific policy initiatives (such as including the arts as basic skills, or including dance and theatre as well as art and music in the required curriculum, or including the arts in credits toward graduation).

2. Testify before local, state, and national legislators and policy developers.
3. Invent appropriate collaborations with state and local education organizations, wedding the arts to their agendas.
4. Develop public information campaigns to inform the public of the need for the arts and the effects of a good arts education.

Bloom and those who collaborated with her helped inspire community and state campaigns to include the arts in state policies regarding what constitutes basic skills (and therefore mandated curriculum) in the 1970s and '80s. Under the auspices of the Fund, which inaugurated its Arts in Education program in 1967, a team of arts and education road warriors traveled the country providing technical assistance in the development of what they termed comprehensive arts in education plans, which inevitably included the fine art of advocacy. To complement the state-by-state efforts supported by the Fund, Bloom and Fund Associate Director Jane Remer formed a League of Cities for the Arts in Education to demonstrate what schools with ambitious and all-encompassing arts programs looked like and how they operated.

The League networked superintendents or other high-status officials from Hartford, Little Rock, Minneapolis, New York, Seattle, and Winston-Salem in the League of Cities for Arts Education. The fund brought the cities together periodically for show-and-tell meetings and common problem-solving sessions. Joining the superintendents at these meetings were the worker bees who helped their districts' schools join arts education objectives with school improvement efforts. As one who represented a League of Cities city, I found the meetings of the consortium and visits to other cities to be a profound personal education. I learned how other school systems worked and how the arts were taught in various places and at different levels around the country. I participated in lengthy conversations regarding curriculum and evaluation approaches, and best of all, I met and traded ideas with some of the most prominent scholars of schooling and school change in the country, such as Robert Stake, John Goodlad, and Ernest Boyer.

The project coordinators were reasonably effective in advocating for arts education, but most of them had no power to insist on the kinds of practices that they knew would help elevate instruction in the arts as provided by both teachers and teaching artists. At times, this resulted in great gaps between rhetorical claims and actual practice.

Jane Remer, Theodore Berger of the New York Foundation for the Arts, and I were a project management troika who steered a network of New York City arts-centered schools to initiate various innovations in professional development, new arts-enhanced curricula, and the skillful employment of artists. As the Project Manager (a term I detested), I was the Board of Education's liaison to the Fund, a counterpart to those from each of the other League cities. I truly learned to value networking as a reinforcement strategy during this period. I also learned that cheerleading is no substitute for the hard work of highly effective instructional practices, and it was disappointing to see the rather limp kinds of teaching that were to exemplify rigorous learning in and through the arts. None of the cities could claim to have actually changed schools, but they could say that with the visibility of the Fund and its identify with one of the great American philanthropies, they were able to help some schools achieve their self-defined missions. Identification with the Fund helped attract other kinds of support from within their school system and the surrounding communities. More important, we kept learning about each other and borrowing ideas that suited us to support our homegrown efforts.

When the Fund was closed prematurely following the sudden death of John D. Rockefeller in 1978, the cause was taken up by other high-profile (and much richer) philanthropic entities and individuals. David Rockefeller Jr., who had already achieved national recognition for his efforts to advocate for the arts and their importance in the education of children and youth during the later days of the JDR3rd Fund, formed a panel of nationally influential and concerned citizens, artists, and educators and convened hearings in key cities around the country where individuals testified about the importance of the arts in education. His organization, The Arts, Education, and Americans, Inc. (AEA), published *Coming to Our Senses: The Significance of Arts for American Education* in 1977 with a great deal of press attention. In 1980, AEA published a series of small monographs designed to help advocates address such key issues as ideas and money, support from local school boards, self-assessment techniques for schools and school districts, and resources (people and places) to support the development of strong arts programs in schools. A decade later, the American Council for the Arts (ACA) commissioned Charles Fowler to do a follow-up, entitled *Can We Rescue the Arts for America's Children: Coming to Our Senses—10 Years Later* (1988). Around this time, I decided to leave the New York City school system and strike out on my own. I took Charles Fowler's idea of "inventing tomorrow" to heart and opened an office as an independent consultant, doing business as C. F. Associates. Leaving the New York City system gave me an opportunity to finish all the course work for my doctorate and line up some very attractive assignments designing arts magnet schools.

As an educator who was closely involved with arts education initiatives, I was invited to serve as a consultant to both the JDR3rd Fund and AEA. For the Fund I traveled several times to Louisville, where a group of arts education advocates had organized and formed pARTners with the support of the Junior League. Sherry Jelsma's deep concern for education in her state led her from arts education advocate to become President of the Kentucky Board of Education, and she is a leader in educational reform in that state. The pARTners founders were particularly interested in getting programs up and running in the public and independent schools of Jefferson County. They also wanted to track the impact of such programs on children's creative thinking and skills at problem solving, which they did using the few and not very precise instruments that were available at the time.

I worked with David Rockefeller Jr. and his very able Executive Director, Margaret Howard, advising them on one of their advocacy initiatives. Howard later advised the Women's City Club as they mounted an advocacy study to support the arts in New York City schools. My work with the JDR3rd Fund and AEA helped launch my new career as an independent consultant. C. F. Associates continues to provide assistance in training, program development, evaluation, and assessment of arts education programs nation-wide.

As the involvement of the Rockefellers waned, two new high-profile organizations took up the banner of arts education. Most prominent was the Getty Foundation, whose Arts Education program officer, Lani Lattin Duke, spent two years surveying the field from top to bottom before designing one of the most influential arts in education initiatives of the latter twentieth century.

Concurrent with the establishment of the U.S. Office of Education's Arts and Humanities office was the creation of the Kennedy Center for the Performing Arts (1965), which had as part of its charge the creation of a national arts education program that could include events that would alert local U.S. Congress men and women of the existence of the arts and the importance of arts education. The Kennedy Center fostered a network of state Alliances for Arts Education, many of which help to shape their states' arts education policies and practices. The 1970s also saw the expansion of state arts councils and their artists in schools programs. Groups with natural affiliations such as nonprofit arts organizations formed advocacy alliances on both a state and national basis (National Association for Artists' Organizations [NAAO], Alliance for the Arts, American Council for the Arts, etc.).

The Getty Center for Education in the Arts, a creation of the J. Paul Getty Trust, followed Bloom's template, gathering of the most prominent art educators and most recognized educational gurus to guide and subsequently endorse what the Getty advocated: Discipline-Based Art Education (DBAE). DBAE became the rallying cry of forward-thinking school districts and arts organizations that craved the very generous grants from Getty. Lani Duke responded to a situation that has plagued art education the way that math tests have plagued the field of mathematics education. Getty grantees developed a variety of art-specific curricula for elementary and secondary school students. As a final contribution to the field before its demise, the Getty Center facilitated the development of a DBAE Curriculum Sampler (1998) and a guide to DBAE (Dobbs, 1998). The extensive publishing program launched by the Getty Center helped inform teachers and parents, in particular, of the issues associated with its four principles and the development of aesthetic sensibilities.

Getty's grant-making process focused on four principles of arts education: production, criticism, aesthetics, and history. Although no one would deny the value of educational practices utilizing the arts or education in the individual arts disciplines, when authorities in the theoretical branches of arts education were sent out by Getty and the NEA to see what was going on in the name of art, music, dance, theatre, and occasionally the literary arts, they reported a plethora of mediocrity where the arts were not given their due instructionally. They saw trite examples of creative work in the making and found that the standards of excellence were well above actual practice. These findings were most influential in formulating the call for arts education reform by Frank Hodsoll when he was chair of the NEA, in May 1988.

Many arts educators were at first hostile to the DBAE orthodoxy, but by the end of the Getty Center's arts education initiatives, most advocates of arts education were grateful for the prominent place the arts were given because of the huge public relations effort that made DBAE a national mantra among arts educators.

Another funding source for learning in and through the arts arose under the sponsorship of Andrew Galef, a successful businessman, and his wife, Bronya, both active arts philanthropists. The Galef Institute founded Different Ways of Knowing (DWOK). Since 1989, DWOK has established programs in major cities across the nation and has won recognition for its work on behalf of learning through the arts.

The role that high-profile foundations have played in supporting and, in many instances, maintaining arts education programs was continued in the 1990s and into the twenty-first century by the Annenberg Foundation. The Annenberg Challenge, a multiyear, very high-profile grant-making program jumped into the arts education arena to meet what they called "a dual challenge: whole-school improvement and arts education" (Annenberg, 6). They awarded three Challenge Grants—one in Minneapolis (Arts for Academic Achievement, administered by the Perpich Center for Arts Education in partnership with the Minneapolis Public Schools) one in New York City (to The Center for Arts Education), and one to the National Arts Education Consortium (Transforming Education through the Arts, TETAC)—with matching funds from the J. Paul Getty Trust. Multiyear Annenbergs were funded through regranting in sites from coast to coast.

Where the Money Is

During the course of the past thirty years, I have occasionally been asked to be a reader for foundations and government grant makers. It has never ceased to amaze me how the same applicants appear year after year, decade after decade. At the same time, I find those that do not apply may well be the most needy school districts in the nation. In order to get most government competitive grants, you have to prove that you are already a winner. Your ducks are in a row. You know what to do and you just need the federal or foundation money to do it better or do more of it. You are willing to jump through the necessary hoops and have the personnel in the back office to drive the paperwork. What is wrong with this picture? Although the neediest school districts receive their portion of Title One funds, designated for schools serving economically disadvantaged communities, and students from poverty or near poverty in schools that are not otherwise needy, these schools rarely get a crack at the prestigious grants unless they have already proven themselves to be fairly effective.

With the election of Ronald Reagan, an energetic attack on the state of education was launched that almost destroyed the Department of Education and the NEA. The policies that resulted from this attack continue to influence the current state of arts education and education through the arts. With the publication in 1983 of the report *A Nation at Risk*, all aspects of education were put on the defensive. Written under the guidance of the National Commission on Excellence in Education, appointed by President Reagan, it recommended demanding instruction in English, mathematics, science, social studies, computer science, and foreign language (the Basics) and the New Basics consisting of the fine and performing arts and vocational education. Of the New Basics, the Commission said "they should demand the same level of performance as the Basics." The report called for "more rigorous and measurable standards and higher expectations for academic performance," more time on learning the New Basics, a longer school day, a detailed strategy for affecting the preparation of teachers, and a desire to "make teaching a more rewarding and respected profession." It also addressed deficits in leadership and fiscal support by proposing strategic steps to take. When *A Nation at Risk* was first published, much more public attention was paid to the criticisms and less to the recommendations, but it is striking to see how many of the recommendations were put into law and Department of Education regulations in subsequent years and with many positive results. The Department of Education actually came out of this contretemps stronger than before the attacks, and more money has flowed into federal and state education budgets in the years since.

Another remarkable document, this time specifically aimed toward reform of arts education, was *Toward Civilization* (National Endowment for the Arts, 1988); it became the Bible for arts education strategists throughout the next decade. *Toward Civilization* was a response to a Congressional mandate that called for a "study of arts education" as part of the reauthorization of the NEA. *Toward Civilization* is an excellent example of how a committee worked to generate a major policy statement although members of the committee varied in power and prerogatives as individuals. The consensus reached by the creators of *Toward Civilization* revealed the difficult road to reform in arts education:

> It cannot be stressed too much that reform in arts education must be undertaken on a long-term basis and measured in decades, not years. We know at this stage of no school district in the country that has included the arts in the curriculum systematically, comprehensively, and sequentially from kindergarten through twelfth grade. The task of restructuring and reforming arts education is therefore more difficult than for subjects traditionally included in the core curriculum. (171)

The report went on to advocate three strategies:

   (i) make the case for arts education,

   (ii) facilitate collaboration among the four sectors concerned with arts education (governance, education, arts, business-producer) to make it a basic and sequential part of school instruction, and

(iii) assist development and distribution of curricular, instructional, and assessment models for the benefit of state and local education authorities.

The report then proceeded to detail nine important steps for the NEA in the years between 1988 through 1998 to take in support of these strategies. The bandwagon was gaining speed, and over the next few years funding patterns from the NEA and the federal government began to reflect these strategies. A look at the NEA website will reveal dozens of partnership programs that it has stimulated.

The NEA took the recommendations of *Toward Civilization* and transformed them into a series of funding strategies and partnership initiatives that stimulated major changes such as:

- States have developed standards and frameworks for what students at various ages and stages should be required to know and do in the four dominant arts disciplines.
- Many states and local school districts have developed assessment procedures designed to help evaluate the teaching of arts education subjects.
- Many states have strengthened their teacher certification requirements for those responsible for teaching the arts.
- Millions of dollars of federal, state, and local nongovernmental funds have been allocated to research the impact of arts education on students, schools, and society.
- The NEA and the U.S. Department of Education have been working together over the past two decades to support research projects regarding the arts and aspects of school reform.
- Partnerships between governmental and private sectors have emerged in order to make the case for arts education as a "fundamental educational responsibility" of society.
- The NEA has expanded its education efforts so that arts education programs constitute 8 to 10 percent of the total grant-making budget.[1]

The U.S. Department of Education followed suit, allocating more and more funds through its formulaic and competitive grants programs. Most recently it has been funding potential models of integrated arts teaching and learning and partnerships between schools and local arts organizations. As a reader of proposals for the Arts in Education Model Development and Dissemination Grants Program, I have been impressed with the sincere tone of some proposals, but dismayed at the shallow thinking of too many other proposals. Some seem to be

---

[1] The percentage is probably much greater considering that Arts for Learning is the primary education category, but educational activities are funded through other categories as well.

written in seclusion by development officers of arts organizations rather than composed as the result of collaborative planning between the groups involved in the ultimate delivery of services. A published list of models that are currently funded by the Office of Innovation and Improvement may be seen at the U.S. Department of Education website [*http://web99.ed.gov*].

In 1989, President Bush (41) met with the nation's governors to reach a consensus regarding a set of National Education Goals. Unlike *A Nation at Risk* or *Toward Civilization*, the summit report did not mention the arts as one of the mandatory areas of instruction. Arts education advocates in organized and individual efforts mounted a successful nationwide campaign to have the arts added to the goals.

Leaders from both the education and arts communities rallied to the cause, as did business leaders who felt that what the workforce needed in the next millennium were men and women with the power to think creatively about both persistent problems in America and those yet undefined. Those of us on various advocacy listservs were inundated with requests to send letters and telephone our legislators and the President so that the situation would be corrected. By 1991, the National Assessment Governing Board approved inclusion of the arts in the National Assessment of Educational Progress, which was to signal to school systems that the arts were finally a legitimate area of the curriculum. By 1994, the National Standards for Arts Education were published and disseminated broadly. States and local districts were able to use this codification of what experts in the four fields considered most important for K–12 students to know and do in what became a template of sorts. According to the Consortium of National Arts Education Organizations, upon completion of secondary school, students should be able to:

- Communicate at a basic level in the four arts disciplines.
- Communicate at a proficient level in at least one art form.
- Analyze works of art according to structural, historical, and cultural perspectives.
- Have an informed acquaintance with exemplary works of art from a variety of cultures and historical periods and understand their place in historical or cultural contexts.
- Cross disciplines to relate various types of arts knowledge and skills.

That was the good news. The more problematic news was that by including the arts as part of a basic education, the arts would have to be assessed just as English, math, science, and social studies were. A national assessment of arts education was administered to a national sample of students in 1997. Many states began to create their own test instruments for assessment of student progress. The results of the National Assessment of Educational Progress (NAEP) test of a sample of eighth graders were predictable. The test tried to show on the one hand that where the arts were taught, students showed ability in responding to, critiquing, and creating satisfactory work products. They also needed to show that where the arts were not taught, students showed a deficit in these earnings. They tried to create a valid and reliable test that would be fair but would not embarrass. The result was that the test was neither very challenging nor very compelling to show the qualitative limitations of much arts education. My quarrel was that the test was an awkward way to make the arts an important element of education for all, and a test of all four disciplines was simply too big a job to be repeated for any kind of longitudinal comparison. Since publication of the NAEP data, Scott Shuler at the Connecticut Department of Education has done a masterful job of aligning assessment with arts teaching. His models have led the field toward upgrading assessment practices.

At the time *Toward Civilization* was published, many of my colleagues voiced concerns at national meetings and in association publications, worrying that undue influence would be exerted by the partner-like relationship between the Getty Trust's Arts in Education program and the NEA. They feared that the two entities were going to eradicate the heart and soul of art education in the name of DBAE (discipline-based art education). They worried that the NEA–Getty partnership was too elitist and misunderstood the dynamics of arts education. Some arts educators had trouble with the notion of "sequential curriculum," interpreting the mandate as counter to the very nature of arts education. Some critics saw the mandate as a conservative–liberal battleground where "high art" was to be given more value than folk or multicultural art, denying children opportunities to see their local experiences as part of an important artistic legacy.

I have to confess that I felt very much like those who criticized both *A Nation at Risk* and *Toward Civilization* and the influential role of Getty. Now I find myself seeing the two documents with greater appreciation and yearn for the presence of Getty within the arts in education universe. The Getty Arts in Education program head, Lani Lattin Duke, had a remarkable capacity to listen to her critics and modify her policies accordingly. She also knew how to enlist critics to share their ideas under the Getty imprimatur. The recommendations from this watershed of policy making continue to make sense, and it is good to see how so many of them have resulted in positive outcomes.

Certainly the research base has broadened considerably because of the call for both parity and exploration of evidence behind the claims for arts in education programs. Recent reports on the influence and effects of arts education on students, such as *Schools, Communities and the Arts* (Welch and Greene, 1995); *Champions of Change* (Fiske, 1999); *Critical Links* (Deasy, 2002); and *Gaining the Arts Advantage* (Longley, 1999), have encouraged advocates. In 1992, U.S. Secretary of Education Lamar Alexander created an America 2000 Arts Education Partnership to act on the recommendations of *Toward Civilization*. He encouraged the formation of the Arts Education Partnership Working Group, led by the Kennedy Center's then chairman, James Wolfensohn, and the Getty Trust's then president, Harold Williams. In 1993, the Group issued the report *The Power of the Arts to Transform Education*. In 1994, the Clinton administration added the arts to the core subjects in the National Education Goals as part of the Goals 2000, which signaled a spate of grant opportunities aligned with the recommendations of the various policy papers mentioned previously. The combined forces of advocates for the arts and arts in education garnered major attention from the two key federal government agencies: the U.S. Department of Education and the National Endowment for the Arts. Not only did advocates impress these two agencies with the importance of arts education, but the agencies found attention to arts education served their purposes as well. Too much attention was cast on the few controversial grants that offended the right wing of the Republican Party. Here was a more benign issue that could help keep the NEA afloat during Congressional scrutiny and opposition. Preparation for the new millennium served as an occasion to launch major arts education initiatives. U.S. Secretary of Education Richard Riley and NEA Chairman Jane Alexander convened more than one hundred national organizations in a Goals 2000 Arts Education Planning Process to address three objectives:

- To affirm the arts as fundamental to quality education and reform.
- To articulate how the arts can contribute to achieving the National Education Goals.
- To identify how individuals and organizations could work together to assure that the arts become a central component of state and local education reform plans.

Participants produced a plan: *The Arts and Education: Partners in Achieving Our National Education Goals*, and recommended "the development of an ongoing partnership among the participating organizations." The U.S. Department of Education and the NEA agreed to support the development of this Goals 2000 Arts Education Partnership. Meanwhile, the USED and NEA entered into a cooperative agreement with the Council of Chief State School Officers and National Assembly of State Arts Agencies to provide administrative support for the Partnership. The Partnership began operations and held its first meeting of participating organizations in October 1995. The agenda for the Partnership was straightforward: to help state education agencies realize the following three goals:

1. State education agencies and school districts should develop consensus on what all students should know in the arts before graduating from high school. The should provide required and optional courses, curricula, and materials to achieve this. The design and media arts should be included as should history, critical analysis, creation and performance.
2. State education agencies, with federal assistance, should develop procedures comparatively to evaluate district and school arts programs in relation to state arts education goals. Local school districts, with federal and state assistance, should do the same based on their curricula.
3. State certifying agencies should strengthen and broaden teacher certification requirements in the arts for all teachers whose responsibilities include the arts.

With the end of the Clinton administration, and the demise of Goals 2000 as the template for school reform, the Partnership could point with pride to having accomplished the three goals. It gained a life extension and was renamed simply the Arts Education Partnership. The Arts Education Partnership continues to collaborate with a variety of education and arts organizations to commission research, provide public information, and convene grassroots partnerships for the purpose of sharing best practices. Among the important studies co-commissioned by the Arts Education Partnership were *Gaining the Arts Advantage*, a compendium of Lessons Learned from School Districts that Value Arts Education; *Champions of Change*: The Impact of the Arts on Learning; and "Good Schools Require the Arts," an attractive advocacy brochure. A complete list of Arts Education Partnership activities and publications can be seen on its website [*www.aep-arts.org*].

There are other national arts education policy-oriented organizations. Americans for the Arts is a membership organization that frequently partners with other organizations such as the National Assembly of State Arts Agencies (NASAA), and the prestigious President's Committee on the Arts and Humanities, which is composed of presidential appointees. It also partners with the Arts Education Partnership. There are also discipline-based arts organizations representing teachers and supervisors of art (National Art Educators Association or NAEA), music (Music Educators National Conference or MENC), dance (National Dance Association or NDA, and National Dance Education Organization or NDEO), and theatre (American Alliance for Theatre and Education or AATE), as well as national organizations for educators of various roles such as the Association for Supervision and Curriculum Development or ASCD, the unions (American Federation of Teachers or AFT, National Education Association or NEA), the elementary and secondary principals' associations, and so on.

With the election of President George Walker Bush (43), a spotlight was trained on education reform once more. This time, a controversial template was ordained in the infamous No Child Left Behind version of the Elementary and Secondary Education Act. Built into the act are several strategies allegedly to make schools more accountable for student performance. In my view, it is a piece of legislation that was too hastily written based on unreliable data in the cause of improving schools. It has hurt arts education deeply by invoking in Title One elementary schools the most rigid requirements. It virtually destroys any opportunity for sequential learning in art and music, much less drama and dance, in the nation's middle schools. Moreover, with the requirements to use so-called scientifically based methods of instruction, it has wrung the creative juices out of many schools that, fearing that they will lose federal funding, have eliminated the arts entirely so that they can practice for the mean high-stakes tests. As states have protested the consequences of No Child Left Behind, and as advocacy groups have mounted their campaigns for revisions and exemptions, it will be interesting to see how long the provisions remain in place.

The one lesson learned in reviewing the history of support for arts education is that the advocacy war never ends. There will always be a tension between the arts and other parts of the curriculum, particularly if the school day remains as ridiculously short as it is. In 1978, at a meeting at the Museum of Modern Art to review the Rockefeller Brothers' arts in education awards program, I made a statement to the audience that the arts will never be safe in schools that are only in session for six hours and twenty minutes (the dominant pattern in the country). Reform advocates have only just begun to press hard for states to fund schools for longer days and longer years with only mixed results. I am not talking about after-school programs that are voluntary in nature and usually disappointing in the numbers of students served. I am talking about a mandatory seven or seven-and-a-half hour day replete with strong arts programming as well as ample time for kids to get rigorous physical exercise.

I keep thinking of those wonderful Japanese schools that I visited when on my Fulbright scholarship. Built around courtyards, after each long and strenuous class period, the doors to the courtyard would fling open and dozens of white-shirted children would bound outside, soccer balls clutched, ready to play vigorously for ten minutes or so before going back into the classroom for another go at English, math, science, social studies, arts and music, and, of course, Japanese. Now there is an idea to copy!

Strategies of 3
Reform:
Partnerships,
Alliances, and
Coalitions

*I*n 1994 I wrote in the *Arts Education Policy Review* that collaborations and partnerships have become ubiquitous during the past fifteen years. That statement is even more true ten years later. Collaborations, partnerships, alliances, and coalitions continue to flavor educational reform efforts with varying degrees of success. Collaborative associations form and reform like waves in the ocean, whether to promote policies and programmatic direction or to provide direct service to schools. Alliances that include executives from corporations and educational organizations to address educational improvement can be found in every state as well as in most cities. They are particularly influential in shaping educational policy, as is the case of the National Alliance of Business [*www.nab.com*], since the future of business still depends on the quality of public school graduates as potential employees. Universities are equally concerned about the quality of high school graduates and have formed numerous partnerships to improve the quality of preparation.

Foundations like to promote collaborative efforts toward addressing educational problems, and it is not unusual to see community foundations support civic partnerships or alliances that advocate changes in educational policies. Individual schools occasionally form an alliance for a common approach to education. The Coalition for Essential Schools [*www.essentialschools .org*], an outgrowth of an alliance between Brown University and the Annenberg Foundation, makes the point well.

In the arts in education world, there are direct service collaborations between foundations and networks of schools such as the A+ Schools alliance with the Kenan Foundation in North Carolina. Housed at the University of North Carolina at Greensboro, the A+ Schools demonstrate how the arts can contribute to high performance in schools through emphasis on both education in the arts and teaching an arts-infused curriculum. Other foundations (e.g., Getty Trust, Galef Foundation, and Annenberg Foundation) have spawned networks of arts rich schools with the same idea in mind. The foundations help launch the networks and provide seed money that is usually matched by other philanthropies and the schools themselves. Schools receive underwriting for activities that an ordinary school district cannot fund such as attending off-site meetings, making site visits, participating in interschool dissemination events, hiring consultants for special services, and so on. There are hundreds, possibly thousands, of partnerships between schools and community-based social service organizations, and there are three-way partnerships between foundations, community-based organizations, and schools such as those forged by JP Morgan Chase's community outreach programs.

A problem with many of the collaborative models is that they are based on a premise that the partnership or networking process or coalition will improve schools. Well, maybe they will, and maybe they won't. It takes more than a network to improve the way a school is administered, although the network members may influence each other for the better. One of the dirty little secrets about networks is that there is usually a screening (application) process in place that eliminates poorly performing schools and spotlights schools that are already on the rise. No one likes to work with failures, and the various arts in education networks are no exception. I remember when I first became a consultant on behalf of a foundation, I was told by a new colleague that foundations did not like to take chances; they did not want to fund failures because it would be difficult to admit doing so to the foundation's trustees. This news really stunned me, because it is precisely on turning around failures that many foundations base their missions in education.

Because many networks are created based on an application procedure, schools that genuinely need improving are the least likely to be included. Failing schools rarely apply for improvement. Linking the arts to general educational improvement—even if one could make a case for it—delimits its purpose. All students should have an arts and culturally rich education. Yet subsidies exist for such programs primarily in the name of educational improvement, and educational improvement usually concentrates on schools in the populations with lower socioeconomic indicators and leaves out a large swath of schools that serve the great economic middle.

Although the arts are marketed as a surefire school improvement strategy, they are reduced to token experiences in many of the lowest-performing schools because the principals and staffs are afraid to take time away from drill and test instruction in preparation for the high-stakes testing that will determine their future status. Heads of low-performing schools are loath to risk deviating from prescribed reading programs and mandated times to accommodate arts programs. Paradoxically, arts advocates have tied their viability to working with schools that need to show ever-rising scores on standardized reading and math tests or state-administered exit exams for high schoolers. That is why Lois Hedland and Ellen Winner were so cautionary in their study of recent research reports that help advocates claim the ameliorative effect of the arts on student performance. They warned advocates not to hang their campaigns on such an ephemeral rationale because if and when research counters the current claims, the fragile arts programs will be thrown away in favor of another promised cure-all.

Paradoxes aside, in arts education, partnerships continue to be hailed as strategies of educational reform. The sad fact is that some partnerships work, and others don't. Some partnerships are not really partnerships but are relationships between a provider of service and a client. Marketing services to schools is a way of life for many arts education organizations, and often in order to keep their organizations afloat, directors will promise kinds of services by artists that cannot be delivered well. Visual artists often have to study up on American history so they can instruct their classes on the construction of a fort during revolutionary times or a mural that depicts historical events when the kids are learning the chronology of the westward movement. The results are frequently stereotypical representations of icons of bygone eras that neither increase understanding of events nor add to the knowledge base of the class. Worse yet, the artistic process is often bastardized to make a quick product for hallway or classroom decoration.

In these cases, sometimes decisions are arrived at collaboratively, but most times the providers indicate their list of services, and the clients select the ones they prefer to buy. Some partnerships last until outside funding runs out; others seem to go on like the Energizer bunny, always able to maintain cordial relationships with funders.

Some partnerships advance the educational agenda, whereas others retard it by providing simplistic services resulting in disappointed ex-partners. Many of the disappointments in partnerships can be avoided if the partners genuinely negotiate the nature of the contracted services. Because of the high financial and public relations stakes with partnerships, however, school leadership takes the course of least resistance. The school tolerates the residency or required meetings in order to get the flashy product or maintain status as a model. The most productive arts collaborations are usually those where the relationships are between equals or where the power relationship is clearly spelled out, as in junior or senior partner. True partners hear each other and accommodate to each other's needs and resources in order to fulfill their common mission. Whereas music and art in elementary and secondary schools have usually been taught by credentialed and appointed teachers, arts in education programs rely heavily on lassoing community arts resources to provide additional personnel to teach an expanded notion of the arts in education. Many of these organizations were founded in the heady days of the 1960s when federal money for partnerships first came into existence (see Chapter 2). Partnerships became even more favorable models for educational reform in subsequent decades as fostered by the large corporate structures that relied on high school and college graduates to enter the workforce. As with all innovations, new networks were created to bring practitioners and funders together to examine their work and plan for future development.

Direct Service (Grassroots) Partnerships

I have evaluated many direct service partnerships, and inevitably I find that the most successful ones involve a true investment of time and expertise by the principal, department chair, and teachers with the arts administrators and teaching artists as collaborating professionals. All have something to say to us as strategists for improvements in schools.

One of the earliest partnerships I studied was New York City's Arts Partners program that ran from 1987 to 1995. Arts Partners was actually a combination of two kinds of partnerships. The first was a meta-partnership created out of an alliance between the Mayor's Office, the Department of Cultural Affairs, the Department of Youth Services, and the New York City Board of Education. Their pooled resources were ably administered by a triumvirate of coordinators representing the major partners' top administrators and the Board of Education's arts unit director. Arts Partners was reviewed monthly by the agencies as well as a major supporter of the partnership, the New York Community Trust.

School-based partnerships spawned direct services to students in selected elementary and middle schools. Arts coordinators (or people acting as such in addition to other roles) from local school districts applied yearly for inclusion in the program, which in turn would allocate funds to successful applicants. Districts could then determine which of their many schools would get Arts Partners programs, and they would then help the schools hire teaching artists employed by one or more organizations approved for this purpose. Two-thirds of the districts became Arts Partners. Arts Partners thrived under the dedicated leadership of the management team, which consisted of Carol Sterling for the Board of Education, Judith York for the Department of Youth Services, and Susan Richardson and then Bill Fears for the Department of Cultural Affairs. Later, Thais Barry was added to the staff to manage professional development programs.

I was asked to evaluate the impact of Arts Partners in the early days of the partnership so that participants could learn along the way what was working and what needed work. There were several official and unofficial purposes in the formation of Arts Partners. Although the official goal of the program was to "restore the arts to elementary and middle schools," it was initially conceived as a strategy to amass some major funding to underwrite artists in schools programs in as many schools as possible. Under the leadership of the four agencies and the project management, however, it became much more than that: It demonstrated how the arts could assist in elevating student performance in academic domains. Moreover, it enhanced the skills of school and district-based administrators in coordinating the various and complex elements of a successful partnership between one or more arts organizations and a school.

My evaluation design was geared toward two objectives: (1) examine the workings of Arts Partners as a potential model of service and (2) explore the relationship between Arts Partners residencies and measures of school improvement. I looked at how the sponsoring agencies worked together as overseers of Arts Partners. Did they help raise the consciousness of the city and the school system within it about the positive contributions arts education makes to the development of students? I observed the way the project management team functioned and made recommendations regarding staffing, roles, and functions. I was asked to show how different facets of the program contributed to educational improvement. I looked at Arts Partners' professional development programs, which were designed to increase pedagogical expertise and just plain "school smarts" for teaching artists. In addition, I explored whether Arts Partners programs had a positive influence on reading skills as measured by the city's standardized tests.

One of my favorite studies conducted while I was evaluator of Arts Partners had to do with the way teaching artists could trigger higher-level thinking while conducting classroom sessions. This study became the basis of my doctoral dissertation and is included as the first of several Targeted Studies in *Schools, Communities and the Arts.* It revealed how certain kinds of transactions between professional teaching artists and students led to visible signs of critical and creative thinking and led to the creation of unique and attractive results in play writing and sculpture and, to a lesser extent, dance and drawing.

The most interesting findings derived from my seven years as Arts Partners evaluator were these:

- Collaborations between the major agencies of a city can provide more opportunities to support arts programming than those that the individual agencies offer by themselves.
- The project management team implemented a complex and dynamic program that served multiple purposes effectively. The team demonstrated a level of effective, proactive leadership that established a high-water mark for future efforts. They showed how representatives from three different agencies could work together for the common good of students by dividing their responsibilities and meeting regularly to pool information.
- The prevalence of arts programs in schools did not depress academic test scores despite time taken away from so-called academic tasks.
- Reading scores in certain low-performing schools went up in classes served by Arts Partners programs and declined in somewhat matched classes that did not have Arts Partners. Teachers claimed the arts experiences helped contribute to test results.
- Professional development sessions for teaching artists were greatly appreciated, especially in reference to classroom management techniques. No evidence was gathered regarding the application of training in classroom workshops.
- The project engendered valuable documentation that added information to the field and provided a steady stream of public information to support continuous advocacy.

Shortly after the original New York Arts Program was started, an unrelated Arts Partners program was created in the Kansas City metropolitan area, the result of a detailed assessment and planning process led by the Greater Kansas City Community Foundation and consultants from The Wolf Organization (now Wolf, Keens & Co.). Four school districts—Kansas City, Missouri; Kansas City, Kansas; and Independence and Raytown, Missouri—agreed to participate in a comprehensive planning process that would result in sequential exposure to all of the arts organizations within the area, including theatre and dance companies, museums, and arts education organizations. That program, administered by Young Audiences of Kansas City, became a model for other Young Audiences chapters and continues to provide a paradigm for school systems wishing to expose their students to a variety of cultural expressions over time.

Our evaluation assignment focused first on examining how the pooling of funds partially provided as an incentive from the Community Trust could provide cost-effective management of diverse services in the arts. We also examined how different arts and cultural organizations responded to this incentive for doing business differently. Before Arts Partners, the Kansas City area schools used mostly parents' association funds and small pots of discretionary dollars to purchase arts programming from the various local arts organizations. In many instances, the contracting process was haphazard, and very little thought was given to a rational arc of residencies and performances that would influence students' understandings of the various arts disciplines. Moreover, there was almost no monitoring of the quality of services, which were in some instances superb and in other instances a waste of everybody's time. The program required intensive planning between school district people and their counterparts at various arts organizations and ultimately resulted in a very satisfying, rational sequence of residencies and performances to elementary and secondary schools. The arts organizations actually gained clients, and the schools were able to plan programs around the Arts Partners' opportunities to gain more educational impact. Because Arts Partners was designed to serve every child in each district, the community could look forward to graduating masses of students who were familiar with the cultural resources in their virtual backyard and, hopefully, ready to become their supporters as participants and audience.

New York's Arts Partners in effect disappeared with the replacement of the Koch mayoral administration by the Giuliani administration. Concurrent with the election of Rudolph Giuliani was the arrival on the scene of the Annenberg Foundation, which, in a collaborative effort with the new mayor, stimulated the formation of the Center for Arts Education as a regranting of Annenberg, Board of Education, and Department of Cultural Affairs funds to support arts education efforts that lead to school reform. One of the first jobs of the center was to raise a 3:1 match of Annenberg money. A number of local foundations stepped up to the plate, making it possible to serve more schools with more money than Arts Partners ever had. Many of the lessons learned by district coordinators in the years of Arts Partners were put into effect with the establishment of the New York City Partners in Education program administered by the Center for Arts Education.

Arts Education Policy Initiatives

When working in a school, the policy-making machinery is not readily visible. One sees the results in announcements of new laws or the creation of reports that chart the course for a specified future, or when one has to hustle to prepare students for new tests. But it is not clear, unless you know what signs to look for, when a policy is in formation and what actions are directly traceable to that policy. I have found that many teachers are reluctant to get involved in policy-making processes that determine their professional behavior. They leave that to their union or their political representatives. Sometimes their lack of involvement contributes to policies that seem to drop down from the sky. Because experienced teachers see program innovations come and go, many of them try not to get too involved—a recipe for disastrous results. Perhaps the next decade will see more teachers doubling as active citizens in their communities, a first step in ensuring better support for educational reform efforts.

Collaborations, partnerships, and alliances help forge policy. That's the way it works in America. A review of the signposts marking major policies affecting educational reform through arts education as well as reform of arts education itself provides a primer for political, social, and educational action. One of the collaborative organizations that have played a visible role in the development of arts education policy is the Arts Education Partnership (AEP), created in the mid-1990s to facilitate some of the recommendations that emerged from the NEA report *Toward Civilization* (as described in Chapter 2, p. 34). AEP started as an arts advocacy effort tied to the Clinton administration's 1994 Educate America Act: Goals 2000. The purpose of the act was:

> to improve learning and teaching by providing a national framework for education reform; to promote the research,

consensus building, and systemic changes needed to ensure equitable educational opportunities and high levels of educational achievement for all students; to provide a framework for reauthorization of all Federal education programs; to promote the development and adoption of a voluntary national system of skill standards and certifications; and for other purposes.

Out of this legislation emerged the Goals 2000 Arts Education Partnership, which later morphed into the Arts Education Partnership. The Partnership is supported by a cooperative agreement with the National Endowment for the Arts (NEA) and the U.S. Department of Education and by the contributions of its participating organizations. It has published monographs and brochures summarizing research related to arts education. A list of partnerships that have been featured in their quarterly meetings and publications may be found on their website: *www.aep-arts.org*. The list includes nationally recognized programs such as the Lincoln Center Institute and small partnerships between local high schools and nearby colleges. Members of AEP gain the advantage of hearing about new funding initiatives early in the game so they can plan proposals appropriately. They also hear about research results before the general audience does and get to meet the key leaders in arts education so they can easily call on them as needed.

There are hundreds of national, state and local networks that help advance the agenda of school reform. A few that are particularly useful to arts advocates are The Teacher Network, the Business Roundtable, and the professional association for educators—Phi Delta Kappa. Other powerful networks stem from the Association for Supervision and Curriculum Development, the Coalition of Essential Schools, the International Network of Performing and Visual Arts Schools and, of course, the Kennedy Center's Alliance for Arts Education affiliates. Advocates for school reform and arts education should check out potential non-educational allies such as the various national organizations that advocate for business development, economic development, civil liberties and civil rights, and protection of minority groups.

A primary partner in school reform is frequently the independent community based organization (CBO). CBOs might be arts in education organizations, such as one of the Young Audience chapters, that specialize in serving a school market. Or they might be arts-producing entities such as the Goodman Theatre in Chicago or Manhattan Theatre Club in New York, where the organization provides theatre education experiences in short residencies to classes of students. Dance companies such as the Alvin Ailey American Dance Theater, the Atlanta Ballet, and the American Ballet Theatre (ABT) have created whole departments to reach out to school audiences and prepare them for understanding their repertoire and the process of creative art in their domains. In most cities, new arts producing organizations pop up regularly. In New York, the astonishing Epic Theatre Center established itself after 9/11 as a producing company with an equally important civic education mission. Epic partners with several New York City high schools in creating productions of importance that speak to the ethical base of civil society. These productions include ancient classics, such as *Antigone* and *Oedipus*, and contemporary plays, such as *Hannah and Martin*.

Presenting organizations also engage in partnerships with schools in programs that relate to their series of performances and exhibitions. Many of these were highlighted in a Dana Foundation publication, *Acts of Achievement: The Role of Performing Arts Centers in Education* (Rich, Polin, and Marcus, 2003).

The traditional arts centers in local communities also see the promise of cooperating with schools to foster educational outreach programs. In large cities, settlement houses with generations of immigrants as their clientele have eagerly latched onto local arts funds and have expanded service to the schools in their communities.

As I reflect on the nature of collaborations that attempt to influence policy, I see a pattern of advocacy partnerships that provides lessons to those who wish to learn how to conduct successful advocacy. These include:

- *Incorporation of the principle of inclusion.* Advocacy coalitions should not be perceived as closed associations but rather as opportunities for like-minded organizations or individuals to participate.
- *Involvement of partners in advocacy action as well as rhetoric.* Organization leaders need to work on their constituents and rally the forces for action. This may involve letter writing campaigns, email blitzes, setting up listservs, responding quickly to crises, and enabling partners to generate new ideas and strategies to fulfill the mission within an organizational framework.
- *Clear visualization of how the collaboration can fulfill its joint mission.* An organization that markets educational programming beyond isolated performances needs to have a workable philosophy regarding the nature of its work with children, and then should stick to it. American Place Theatre's Board and Executive

Staff decided to cease creating full productions for an adult subscription audience and stick to its educational programming for
teenagers exclusively. By doing so, it changed from an arts organization that does educational programming to an arts in education organization with the highest artistic standards. Its programs
depend on professional actors and playwrights who know how to
work with students or, in the Lit to Life program, may know how
to construct and direct one-hour play versions of various strong
novels. That's who they are. That's what they stand for.

- *Full-time staff.* An organization that plans to exist for more than a
moment needs a full-time staff to keep the education programs
on course. The staff may be one or more persons, but it must be
adequate to the effort of reaching out to schools or everyone is
wasting time. Arts education partnerships are only as good as the
staffs that carry out partnership goals. The staff must include people with both artistic and educational expertise or they end up
with programs that suffer in one area or the other. Most of the
programs send artists affiliated with their organization into classrooms. If there is no expertise on educational issues within the
organization, then there is no one to help an artist who is having
problems in the classroom. If the artistic work initiated in the
classroom is mediocre and unchallenging, someone has to be
there to recognize the problem and intervene accordingly. Teachers won't generally complain; they would rather just "get it over
with," or just complain among each other. It is up to the organization to oversee its own programs and be prepared to take
action when programs fall below par.

- *Adequate support within the organization.* There is no point in trying to develop an effective arts in education partnership or array
of services if this action is not clearly supported by the Board and
senior artistic staff of the organization. It is not effective to have
education programs bootlegged into theatre and dance companies, museums, or musical ensembles if the programs are not
part of a clearly stated mission exemplified by an appropriate
budget and budget-making process. When education is a prominent part of an artistic enterprise, such as the Epic Theatre Center
in New York, all kinds of symbiotic programming can emerge.
Only recently, Epic was preparing its forthcoming production of
Hannah and Martin, a play based on intimate correspondence
between philosophers Hannah Arendt and Martin Heidegger,
starring David Strathairn and Melissa Friedman. This off-
Broadway company held its rehearsals in the black box theater

of its educational partner, Talents Unlimited High School. Period by period, classes sat in and watched the rehearsals, adding their insights for use by the director and actors. The experience, so intellectually and emotionally demanding, impressed both students and actors and reinforced the reason they are partners.

- *Appropriate budget.* The organization must have enough money (either earned or provided through grants) to maintain a staff, a work environment, and dollars to provide materials and supplies pertinent to programs. In addition, the budget should include money to hire experts to periodically help in strategic planning and evaluation. The budget should include meeting expenses as well as some wiggle room to take care of small, unanticipated needs. Too often the education program is seen as a cash cow for the main artistic enterprise. While a program might, under certain circumstances, contribute to the organization's operating expenses, it cannot be at the expense of the quality of the education program. If an organization cannot afford an education program, it should not have one.
- *Ongoing documentation and evaluation.* Arts organizations are always in need of proving their effectiveness for funders and clients. They also need to keep an eye on their work for their own control over quality. It is important that they build into all programs a system for evaluating the effectiveness of their work and create a capacity for selected documentation, whether high or low tech, on a cyclical basis.

Some arts organizations that have school outreach programs may say that these characteristics are difficult to support, particularly the staff and budget items. And I say, don't try to do what you cannot afford to do well. The Pan Asian Theatre in New York is a wonderful small theatre group that offers outstanding productions of Asian and Asian-American plays in New York. Occasionally they do a play with no particular reference to Asian setting or issue. This theatre group would love to do more ambitious educational programming to support the performances they offer for student audiences. But it cannot afford to do more than present the play, develop educational materials to support the experience for students, and hold a post performance discussion. They have no full-time education director and so, wisely, until they can raise the money to underwrite a full-blown education program, they stick to what they can afford.

Some arts organizations offer rosters of artists to perform or conduct residencies and workshops in schools. Prime among them are the thirty-five or so chapters of Young Audiences, Inc. These organizations hire professional artists to work under their banner, providing oversight and subsidizing costs through their fundraising.

Local arts councils and centers for the arts often investigate partnerships with schools in their communities. These organizations need to be clear regarding how the artists they sponsor approach the arts, particularly how they approach the process of integrating the arts into other aspects of the curriculum. I have seen programs where professional artists have taken classrooms of students to the highest levels of artistry simply by using methods that are akin to the production of professional work. I have also seen programs where the artists try to present foolproof art-making projects that result in a product but that violate some of the most basic creative principles in their field. Arts in education organizations have to ensure that their artists represent the highest form of creative work; otherwise they offer nothing that could not be done within the regular operation of the school. I have spoken with many artists who say that they have never been observed by staff from the sponsoring agency. How can arts organizations stand behind their programs if they do not observe them periodically?

Schools that participate in successful partnerships also have characteristics that foretell their quality:

- *Keeping promises through thorough and recurrent planning.* Schools need to keep their promises when they plan with arts organizations. If they are going to provide release time for teachers, they need to come through with that promise. If they are going to provide a particular performance space or studio in which to work, they need to do so. If they promise a change of schedule to allow double periods for sessions, then they have to do so. The biggest stumbling block for schools that fail to deliver their promises is inadequate and insufficient planning. This is frequently a budget item. Planning needs to happen not just once but over time. Planners should allocate appropriate time to complete planning tasks well. Schools need to ensure that the people who need to get together have enough paid time to do their work well.
- *Appropriate facilities.* Schools without adequate space for full-blown dance programs should consult with professional dance companies for advice regarding how to do good work within the constraints of existing facilities. There are many ways to provide dance as a break from the passive classes kids endure for most of the school day, but pushing back the desks in the usual classroom is not a favorite. Creative dancers have found all kinds of ways to use rotten space to do their work, but the compromises on safety

and instructional ambitions generally dissipate whatever values the dance classes could offer. I would rather have no dance in a school without adequate space than see students and instructors crammed into a classroom already crowded with desks, chairs, bookbags, aquaria, and a zillion other objects. Sometimes the best option is to run a dance program as an extension of the school day rather than within the school day, taking advantage of space that is usually restricted during normal hours.

As a strategy for reform, collaboration can yield very important results, or it can lead to catastrophes large and small. The wise advocates of arts education as a vehicle supporting school reform should best review this section before promising to deliver educational goals beyond their reach.

Artists in Education 4

*A*rtists as Teaching Partners

A Professional artists, either affiliated with an organization or independent, have become allies of teachers who are dedicated to delivering a broad and more complex approach to education in and through the arts. The role of artists in schools has expanded greatly from the time when a few writers and educators gathered together to form the Teachers and Writers Collaborative. They wanted to do their part to repair the dismal lack of good instruction in writing in New York City's public schools some thirty years ago. They wanted to teach kids the way they, as youngsters, would have wanted to be taught: to craft language instead of parsing it; to explore meaning and metaphor based on a desire to say what the kids wanted to say rather than superimpose uninspired topics to write about. These writers also wanted to engage in ongoing dialogue with kids through their writing, a luxury not often afforded by teachers in middle and high schools with five classes' worth of papers to correct.

> Because they were writers they addressed themselves initially to what they saw as disastrous shortcomings in the English curriculum; ... their concern for

51

language and the ways that schools traditionally choked off students creative, alive, use of language was only a metaphorical starting-point for larger concerns about educational tracking and racial and social injustices that seemed to be taking place in the schools. The writers' (and later the other artists') idea was that by going into the schools, they could both lend support to the students' "authentic" voices and cultures, while taking students further through professional guidance in art-making activities—at the same time helping to bring about a more enjoyable, unrepressed school environment. (Lopate)

One day while I was reviewing geographical facts of the Caribbean Basin with my eighth grade Core class for a forthcoming test, the door opened and there stood my supervisor with a visitor in tow.

"May we sit in?" Edythe Gaines asked.

"Of course," I answered, smiling.

"Good. Class, this is David Henderson. He is a poet. Would you like to hear his poetry next period?" she asked me and my class. A chorus of yays, cheers, and applause responded—anything to avoid the end-of-unit test!

"We would love to," I said in my prim, early-1960s notion of a twenty-something teacher in charge.

Edythe suggested that we finish our review and then make our way to the library, where we would join a few other classes to hear Henderson the poet. I recall with a blush how boring my review lesson must have seemed to Henderson. I learned later that he was from the newly established Teachers and Writers Collaborative out of Columbia University, and here I was leading the eighth graders through a Simple Simon of geography facts as laid out in a simplistic semifactual textbook. (Oh, how I would love to reteach Caribbean geography today. How differently I would do it with videotapes of musical and dance performances and varied kinds of maps from the Internet and audiotapes of regional music ready for analysis; with plans for seeing a live performance of Ballet Hispanico or Flamenco-Vivo! And readings from some of the fine Caribbean writers who were yet to be published: Julia Alvarez ,Sandra Cisneros, Edwidge Danicat, and Christine Garcia, among others. With classes in various dances of the African Diaspora and culminating with an in-class performance by my former student, Tiberio Nascimento, famous American Brazilian guitarist!)

We herded ourselves to the library to hear David. He stood, he bowed, and he began to read his verses in a stentorian, theatrical voice. I looked around at my students. They were totally flummoxed! They did not understand the poetry; they could not relate to the process or the poet. They were polite—weeks of training ensured that—but the experience was lost on them. Only later did I discover that David was part of a great experiment documented so well by Philip Lopate[1] that began a movement that is now international in scope[2] and a virtually permanent institution in thousands of schools across America.

I didn't know who David Henderson was (I do now![3]) and I had no time to find out, much less to prepare my students for what they were about to attend. Every rule and advisory that has ever been written regarding introducing an artist to a class was violated, which undermined the good intentions that governed such an opportunity for the students. What a wasted opportunity! Had I but known who he was, what his poetry was about, and what he was interested in reading to the students, I could have provided just the right context for his appearance. We learn from the mistakes of ourselves and others. David continues to haunt me whenever I speak about the pros and cons of artists in classrooms.

Compare the Henderson experience with a residency I helped design combining Diane Coburn Bruning, an extraordinary dancer and choreographer, founder of the Chamber Dance Project, with Adrienne Garnett, a uniquely energetic, creative fine arts teacher at New Rochelle High School. The three of us decided that Adrienne's advanced art students needed to think about the relationship between the creation of a dance and the creation of a drawing. We wanted them to reflect on such common issues as energy, gesture, movement, and, ultimately, message. Diane brought videotapes of her choreography as well as some tubes (shades of Martha Graham) and bolts of cloth with which she and the students experimented. Adrienne set up drawing boards, various kinds of drawing tools, and sketch pads so that as Diane and a few volunteers played with the tubes and fabric, using the shapes and moves associated with modern ballet, the students drew what they saw and what they felt as they observed the dancers. The drawings were wonderful: full of life, flashes on paper that complemented the bursts of energy on the stu-

---

[1] *Journal of a Living Experiment*, edited and with commentary by Phillip Lopate. Teachers & Writers Collaborative. 1979.

[2] See the website for Creative Communities, the European effort to inform and advocate started by Jennifer Williams and the British-American Council on the Arts [*www.creativecommunities.org*].

[3] Henderson is an award-winning African-American poet whose political and social ideas infuse his work. He first gained prominence in the 1960s and presaged the poetry of the hip-hop generation.

dio's improvised stage. The experience launched a detailed discussion of the relationship of one art domain to another, of the payoff each artist gets from collaborating across domains.

As the appearance of teaching artists or artist teachers became more commonplace, funded by local and state arts councils as well as private and corporate foundations, it became obvious that artists needed advice as they began to craft their new careers as adjunct teachers. Advice to artists, regardless of their medium of professionalism, tends to fall into several categories:

- Ages and stages of child and adolescent development and teaching implications.
- How to manage a classroom—an examination of how to work with a group as opposed to with individuals; understanding how to relate to the very young, the middle school, and high school populations.
- How to develop what I call a teaching scenario—its place within a unit and lesson plan.
- How to develop a means of finding out whether what has been taught has been learned (an evaluation plan).
- How to research best practices in order to learn from those who have preceded you in this work.
- How to prepare mind and body for the exigencies of teaching large classes in public elementary and high schools.
- How to negotiate roles and functions of team teaching with teachers.
- How to select a common theme or purpose in tandem with teachers.
- How and when to call for help.

In the early days of artists in schools, these issues popped up daily because artists and school people were encountering them for the first time. When need for help was obvious, there was a tendency to do it hastily and superficially or to rely on the advice of artists with reputations but not necessarily with the right advice. I remember one artist encouraging his workshop participants to think of teaching in a series of shibboleths: young kids have short attention spans, don't involve the teachers, create something that is quick, easy, and attractive for a quick win, and so on. This kind of advice added to the criticism by some in education that teaching artists were just fast-track itinerant teachers who preferred not to go through the rigmarole of getting certified. What artists needed then and still need today before they start work are strategies that will help them preserve their identity as adjuncts, guests, special visitors with special gifts to share. There are some model artist training programs throughout the country, many of them sponsored by state arts councils, others sponsored by universities in collaboration with arts organizations. The good ones take enough time to do the job well, and they follow up their seminar-type work with a mentoring program or its equivalent that gives trainees an opportunity to practice more effective techniques before a friendly critic who can feedback to them the answer to "how am I doing?"

Most artists who appear in classrooms today do so because they are sponsored by a not-for-profit arts organization of some kind. And most organizations that are serious about maintaining their artists in schools programs provide some kind of orientation and training. In the old days of Arts Partners (see previous chapter), professional development stipends were offered to artists, which made it more attractive for freelancers to attend the whole series. The topics were those mentioned earlier in this chapter, and discussion leaders were experienced *and* successful teachers, psychologists specializing in how children and adolescents learn, peer artists with reputations for expertise in curriculum or instructional techniques, and individuals with a firm grip on classroom management. The series always worked best for those artists who attended each one sequentially, but there was no way that Arts Partners could follow up training with on-site observations. Consequently, one of the most important ingredients of successful training was missing. It is one thing to provide advice and some role-plays to address problems that artists encounter. But nothing replaces observations of work sessions with an opportunity for constructive feedback. Schools that embrace the notion of Critical Friends (adapted from a practice common to the Coalition of Essential Schools) might be able to provide that kind of feedback to teaching artists, but it requires a willingness on the part of the artist to participate and the availability of a Critical Friends chapter to provide the feedback.

Teaching Artists as Teacher Trainers

A string tied to many grants given to teaching artists or arts organizations requires teaching artists to set aside time to train teachers. Here again, we find a good idea that requires rethinking. The original idea was to give teachers some background in the work that the artist was to present with the thought that the teacher could carry on after the artist's departure. In my experience, this rarely happens, unless the teacher is already comfortable with the artistic medium, which actually happened more often than one might expect. Teachers are frequently asked to volunteer to work with an artist, which would explain their affinity with the art form. It is, however, unrealistic to think that a warmup and dance class is going to make a huge difference or even a small difference to people who have (1) never taken a dance class in their lives, (2) would still not feel comfortable leading a dance class for their students, and (3) would not have the skills, knowledge, or judgment to lead a quality experience.

Teaching artists are increasingly realizing that their role as teacher-trainers needs to be much more circumscribed. They are most valuable when they teach about their art and lead teachers through the process that students will go through in the residency. In the process of experiencing what the students will experience, both artist and teacher can begin to anticipate some of the challenges and issues that might arise and prepare strategies to meet them. Combining "talk abouts" with art making gives teachers an opportunity to gain some confidence and also some insight about the crucial role decision making, problem solving, and creative thinking should play in the art-making process.

There is something attitudinal requiring a teaching artist to train teachers. The more propitious descriptive phrase might be to share with teachers something about what they do as artists. Somehow, the notion of teaching artists teaching teachers how to teach what the artist took years of study to learn does not seem quite right. Just as teaching artists are not equipped to teach after participation in a two-session workshop, so teachers of academic subjects are rarely equipped to teach art or music, or dance or drama, in their classrooms as a result of a teacher's workshop with the resident artist.

That said, I remember vividly when I was managing the Arts in General Education (AGE) project in New York City, Walter Nicks, an outstanding modern dancer, invited the teachers from PS 98, where he was in residence as a movement specialist (NEA nomenclature for a single dancer as opposed to a company in residence), to volunteer for a lunchtime dance class. He had almost the whole faculty in the gym, taking class just for the fun of it! And it was a wonderful experience for everyone. He wasn't teaching the teachers how to teach dance; he wasn't expecting that those who took a class were going to become dancers; he was just giving them the kind of class that beginners take, and it was up to the teachers to make of it what they wanted. The teachers bonded with Nicky and started attending performances of not only Nicky's company, but other companies as well. A perfect residency.

When Pauline Koner, eminent modern dancer in her day, was in residence with her company in New Rochelle's Webster School, the teachers filed into the library for a seminar with her. There they learned what it was like to be the principal dancer for Jose Limon, how he choreographed his most famous dances "on" her, and how she learned to walk on the icy streets of Moscow in the 1930s when she was performing there ("take very tiny steps, almost gliding"). The teachers had a wonderful time; they asked lots of intelligent questions, and they left the seminar enthused about Pauline, her company, and modern dance.

Tony Randall made it a habit when he inaugurated the National Actors Theatre to speak with the fifteen or so regulars who were invited to bring their classes to the theatre to see one of the classic plays that the company presented. He was the perfect trainer providing anecdotes about the play, discussing the playwright, the experience of being directed in the play, and the history of the play when originally produced. The teachers felt like honored guests and warmed up to their famous host in short order. Randall felt that it was as important for the actors to play to students as it was to play for adult audiences. They responded with such exuberance to each play's climactic moments that they energized the actors on stage to even greater heights. This was in part a result of the way Tony prepared the teachers, who then prepared their students for the experience.

Recently, under the auspices of the Lincoln Center Theatre, Matthew Dakins, dramaturg and director of the recently produced *Henry IV* (Parts One and Two), chatted with a group of teachers as part of the Lincoln Center Theatre's network of high school English teachers with whom they work all year. He talked about his own tasks as adaptor of Shakespeare's two history plays into one and then worked with the teachers on one page of a scene. He conducted that part of the session as he would with actors reading the scene aloud for the first time. In so doing, he helped teachers see aspects of the play, the forthcoming performance, and their role as teachers in brand-new ways. Teachers left the experience filled with excitement about how to translate their experience to their students before attending the performance. That might not be training, but it was an exhilarating orientation process.

Teaching Artists as Negotiators

One of the problems that artists continually face when assigned to a school is how to negotiate the details of their assignment for mutual satisfaction. Artists need to have the courage to say no when a request is inappropriate. If a school wants to do a drama unit on Shakespeare, and the artist is not well versed in Shakespeare, no amount of winging it is going to meet high standards. If an artist is a painter and is asked to do a sculpture project, it may be time to say, "I don't do sculptures." It is unfair to the school, the students, and most important to the artists to have to try to work outside of their areas of expertise. At the same time, artists need to contribute to the negotiation by suggesting alternative ideas that are within their area of expertise, and their sponsoring organizations need to be supportive. Both need to understand that the best work evolves from ideas that students suggest—ideas that reflect what is on their minds. Whenever possible, students need to have input regarding the content of the residency.

Too often artists, out of their strong desire to please, are trapped into agreeing to do things against their better judgment. For example, they are asked to do a project with twice as many youngsters as they can handle. Or they are asked to write, produce, and perform a musical play in five sessions (I kid you not!). Or, because they happen to be actors, for example, they are asked to design sets, create lighting, or perform other theatre-related tasks beyond their expertise. Saying no does not mean that artists will lose their assignment; it just gives them and the school an opportunity to negotiate a better project. Saying no is not just about negotiating with schools. Sometimes artists have to say no to their sponsoring organization when they are asked to do something that is out of their area of interest or expertise. At the same time, they need to be free to suggest alternatives instead of just saying no.

Negotiating Planning Time and Content

Artists need to make sure that planning time is set aside not just for figuring out logistics, schedules, test dates, and so on, but for content, theme, procedures, and anticipated outcomes as well. Too often, a planning period is set aside equivalent to a class period (forty minutes maximum), which is hardly enough time to describe what the residency could address. Artists and teachers leave the session puzzled if not frustrated about what is in store for them if it is their first time working together. Artists may assume that teachers will be eager to talk on the phone at night about the impending assignment. This is not always so, especially before artists and teachers get to know each other. Teachers may assume that the artist comes with a bag of tricks and the teachers just have to sit back and stay out of the way. This kind of behavior can be misunderstood as hostile to the artist. Artists and teachers need to negotiate their roles and tell each other how they would prefer to work in a shared classroom. Artists and teachers need to work through the ways that an artist's work with students contributes to the learnings for which the teacher is ultimately responsible. If the idea is that students will learn more history after exploring Shakespeare's *Henry IV*, then artist and teacher have to identify the specifics that students will be responsible for knowing as a result of both the artist's and teacher's instruction.

The Artist's Teaching Style

Artists as well as teachers are easily seduced into showing off. Performing artists are used to taking center stage in their professional life. This can, however, undermine the purpose of the residency when the intention is to help students find their own creative voices. Artists need to check their work as a classroom resource and make sure the kids are getting their own practice at creative problem solving. To be a good teacher, the students have to be center stage, and the strong resident artists will encourage strong student performances rather than perform themselves. Similarly, visual artists are used to conceptualizing their own work; the hardest part of their work with students is to share the process of conceptualization so that the work is as much generated conceptually by the students as it is fabricated by them. Neither of the previous statements is meant to suggest that teaching artists should not demonstrate their own artistry; that is an essential requirement of a resident artist. But the demonstration needs to be tempered with the understanding that the bulk of the work is about the kids, not the artists.

Recently I moderated a panel of educators and artists who work in Queens, New York. The topic was "Process vs. Product: A false dichotomy?" What ensued was an illuminating conversation in which artist panelists made it very clear that good process can be, in a way, its own product. They warned that the product must emerge from good process and must not be manufactured just to satisfy some external requirement. They were responding to a frequent situation found in schools where there is almost a hysterical demand for a polished performance regardless of how little preparation has been scheduled. They feel a tension between wanting to engage youngsters in a good and satisfying creative arts process under the baleful eyes of school administrators who want to make sure they have something to show off for the parents. If time is spent in negotiations (see previous section), this tension can be resolved to everyone's satisfaction, particularly if the artist thinks ahead of time about what kinds of processes that are intrinsic to the art form can be integrated into the classroom experience and result in some definitive result that is a natural and appropriate outcome of the process.

Many teachers and school administrators want a tangible outcome from a residency that they can point to with pride as a sign of the outstanding experience just completed. The product may be a performance or a mural or a completed videotape documentary. It may involve a gallery show or a concert—an outward sign of good learning, a kind of closure to an extended experience that signals to all that students worked hard and well on a specific project and have achieved excellent results. If the product is a showing of a work-in-progress because of time and space constraints, that's fine, but the setting for showing a work-in-progress must be suitable. An auditorium is not usually suitable, unless the audience is small and the whole tone is informal. I am much happier seeing plays-in-progress acted in a staged reading by professionals than I am seeing sketchy plays performed by lightly rehearsed students to a full audience.

Dancers involved in AileyCamp confronted this issue early in the development of the camps. The nature of AileyCamp is to attract youngsters who want to dance, not youngsters who want to be professional dancers someday. The dance instructors—all professionals—were used to choreographing for dancers with background and skill in ballet, modern, jazz, African dance, or tap. Their challenge was to devise appropriate choreography that could be learned as part of the fun and rehearsed so that the kids looked good, culminating in a big end-of-season performance for parents, friends, and, of course, funders. Their solution was to teach the fundamentals for four weeks of camp, and during the last two weeks of the six-week season, to conduct rigorous rehearsals of choreographed pieces that worked within the limitations of the campers but were sufficiently challenging to be artful. This is not always as easy as it sounds. There is a fine line between simple and unchallenging, between challenging and impossible to learn.

AileyCamp instructors seem to have found a middle ground, as have the choreographers of several other dance in education organizations such as Jacques d'Amboise's National Dance Institute. They know how to push the students to higher levels of effort and artistry, but they are mindful of the constraints of age, physical strength, coordination, and other factors that help define their instructional parameters.

A satisfying example of how the creative process was preserved and yet resulted in a product that met the requirements of the school was born of a partnership between New Rochelle High School and the erstwhile East Coast Arts Centre, a local professional theatre that specialized in incubating young playwrights. Reading plays as literature was part of the high school curriculum, but writing plays in order to understand better how plays are conceived and constructed was a rare opportunity. Professional playwrights and directors selected by Joe Cacacci, East Coast founder and artistic director, were hired to work with an English class guided by gifted English teacher Leslie Herzfeld. Then professional actors were hired to perform the plays-in-progress for parents and friends at the New Rochelle Public Library's theater. One of the young playwrights who had been majoring in "hall wandering" found his creative home in this workshop. He wrote a moving play about a young black caddy at a posh Westchester country club. It was a sensation when performed. For the first time in his high school career, he was recognized as a valuable someone. He not only began to come to the writing class regularly, but also started to attend all of his other classes. For the first time in his four years in high school, he got instant positive recognition from the principal and other teachers as a result of his success as a playwright. It was inspiring to see him assume the mantle of *auteur*.

Not long ago, I happened to observe musical plays-in-progress developed by upper elementary school students who were coached by artists from Making Books Sing, producer of musical plays derived from classics in children's literature. Children were learning the art of transformation by converting books of their choice into plays with music composed in collaboration with a teaching composer. The classroom teacher had been involved in selecting the books for children to consider for the project and had worked with the children between visits by their resident artists. The observation reminded me how effective it is when artists collaborate with teachers to engage kids in a long-term, demanding creative experience.

Artists in Other Domains

Sometimes artists are assigned to a class that deals specifically with their art specialty or discipline. A sculptor who works with special materials might work in an art class with a teacher whose experience with the materials is scant. Such was the case when Jon Snow worked with the art teacher at a Queens junior high school. He was used to working large, with chicken wire and plaster of Paris, and all the tools that go with that, whereas she was predominantly a painter. Together they planned a huge sculpture project that introduced their students to a whole new approach to creating objects.

Most often, however, an artist will be hired to infuse the arts into an academic subject currently under study by the classes assigned to them. The fifth grade is studying Egypt, so the artist is asked to help the kids construct an Egyptian tomb. The first grade is studying their community, so the artist is asked to develop a project that reinforces learning about community. A school is planning a celebration of Martin Luther King Jr. Day, so would the artist please develop a script that could be performed for the occasion? And rehearse the kids for the performance? The math class is composed of kids who do not test well in math. Will the artist help the kids do better in the math class by devising a project that will accomplish that end?

Bobbi Abrams, now working in Florida, was asked to enhance children's understanding of Peruvian culture by working with class-room teachers in PS 46 in Queens on sculptures taken from decorative motifs found in the social studies textbooks. She created a soapstone studio for the children with the appropriate tools and materials and helped the youngsters work in a medium that was brand new to them. The results were stunning and highly referential to the work the students had been doing with their classroom teacher.

Watching Jon Snow, sculptor, photographer, and pied piper, work with high school art students gave me an opportunity to see how the academic can infuse the arts. Students were asked to create visual statements of ideas they had learned in other subjects—quite a switch! Kids conceived their projects in groups but had the option to realize their work in groups or as individuals.

What fun it was to see Diane Coburn Bruning take some important mathematical concepts found in the middle school curriculum and use them as choreographic frames. With Diane, part of the fun was watch-ing her direct a class of teachers to follow a virtual play sheet that involved addition, subtraction, geometry, and algebra to music!

A particularly stimulating example of the arts infusing the social studies curriculum was a project that was both artistically and aca-demically meaningful to the teachers and fourth and fifth grade stu-dents of PS 166 in Manhattan. The company was preparing a new ballet choreographed by Pedro Ruiz. Ruiz used as his inspiration memories of country life in pre-Castro Cuba. His ballet included scenes of Cuban *campesinos* engaged in the daily activities that marked the growing and reaping seasons, from sunup to sundown. A cadre of Ballet Hispanico teaching artists, former members of the company now retired, put the youngsters through a series of creative dance exercises that eventually led to their own echoes of Ruiz's dances. Meanwhile, classroom teachers used the residency as an occasion to teach about Cuba, its history and geography, its place in the Caribbean, and its relationship to America, making good use of the Cuban presence in their neighborhood on the upper west side of Manhattan. Together, teaching artists and classroom teachers wove an integrated arts study that set a high-water mark for dance in education. At the final performance of the student dances, one could say "good art, good education!"

The best work that artists do under the aegis of an arts-integrated mandate is a result of planning for natural connections. Recognizing that the arts have a natural connection to other areas of learning, artists need to plumb those natural connections rather than construct superficial and frequently incorrect exercises. After all, the arts are a part of all other subjects. Only in school are they separate! It should be natural to consider ways in which science and aesthetics merge whether working with photography, paint, synthesizers, or rhythm instruments. It should be natural to introduce anatomy when conducting a dance class. Sometimes schools are tempted to force an unholy alliance between art and an academic objective. This sometimes puts an artist in a quandary. How to teach math through dance? In my mind, the answer is don't! But you might allude to math where it is natural to do so. Counting is a basic requirement for dancers. Establishing shapes, geometrical or otherwise, is a concern of choreographers. The danger comes when the artist is expected to teach students the math curriculum. Let the math teacher work on that problem.

With the standards movement so dominant in today's educational environment, it is important that artists learn to cast their activities in a way that conforms to the language standards as used by schools. For example, a theatre artist might engage in the following activities, typical of what I see in schools:

- The artist assembled several monologues and dialogues selected from acclaimed plays from worldwide theatre traditions appropriate to the class.
- After showing the kids how to warm up their "instrument" (i.e., their bodies and voices), he shared with them his technique for preparing a scene: how he thought about the character, how he tried to walk like the character, how he tried to construct that character's family and history.
- He demonstrated how he would read a scene for the first time.

- Then he gave each child or group of children a scene to study, either a monologue or a dialogue. Some kids worked by themselves. Others worked in twos or threes.
- While the artist worked with one set of kids, the teacher worked with another, having planned together ahead of time so they did not work at cross purposes.
- When the kids had enough time to work through their scenes, the artist showed them how to block the scenes for a "reading," and then he rehearsed them for their "performance."
- At the end of the performances of monologues and dialogues, the students reflected on what they had learned, how they had achieved their best work, and what next steps would be appropriate for further learning.

If one were to translate this scenario into National English Language Arts Standards, it might go something like this:

1. Students will understand the basic features of a reading.
2. Students will apply their knowledge of word origins and word relationships, as well as historical and literary context clues, to interpret text.
3. Students will read and understand grade-level-appropriate material. They describe and connect the essential ideas, arguments, and perspectives of text.
4. Students will read and respond to historically or culturally significant works of world literature.

Details regarding the reading skills are found subordinate to the overarching objectives, and wise teaching artists will appropriate the language and juxtapose it next to their scenarios like this:

Figure 4–1   A Planning Format

Playwriting Unit	
A Collaborative Teaching Scenario	
(Developed by Joe Orton, Artist in Residence, and Linda Lovely, Eighth-Grade English Teacher)	
Arts infused teaching scenario	English Language Arts Standards
Activities (Describe)	Include specific references
Activities (Describe)	Include specific references
Activities (Describe)	Include specific references
Specific references: Cite texts, other materials	
Evaluative instruments, procedures: Cite tests, rubrics for demonstrations, etc.	

What About Discipline: How to Get It, How to Keep It?

I have always believed that if a class is disorderly, resisting any effort to quiet down and get ready to work, then the problem most likely is with the teacher and events that long preceded the arrival of the artist. If the class is orderly at the start and then discipline breaks down, it is probably because of the way the teaching artist has structured the scenario or the way the teacher manages the many elements requiring his or her attention.

There are many good handbooks on classroom management, maintaining positive discipline, and keeping students on task in a productive environment. The Association for Supervision and Curriculum Development (ASCD) has published dozens of articles and books on the topic of classroom management [*www.ascd.org*], and other publishers such as Lawrence Erlbaum Associates are a good resource of books on the subject. In addition, Erlbaum publishes the *Teaching Artist Journal*, edited by Eric Booth. There are several articles in the two volumes in print that discuss issues of classroom management.

As an arts education administrator, I was often distracted from seeing the best collaborations in order to solve problems with the most difficult collaborations. It is tempting to let the problem sites overshadow the successful ones, but one must resist the impulse. I remain a firm supporter of artists in schools as collaborators, as resources for professional development of teachers, and as creative agents in place in schools that need an uplift from daily routines. But as a problem solver, I remain adamant that arts organizations need to monitor the work of their artists in the field and have the in-house expertise or ability to hire consultants to help artists overcome obstacles to effective practice. Here are the things that drive a teacher crazy:

- Artists do not come on time to school, or to class.
- Artists do not share what they are going to do nor do they ask the teacher to share.
- Artists fly out of the classroom at the end of the period.
- Artists expect everything to be ready for them, which means cutting time from reading/math.
- Artists do not know how to control the class.
- Artists don't know how to come to closure at the end of the period.

Here are some things that drive artists crazy:

- Teachers are never ready when the artist comes in to teach.
- The room is always crowded, cluttered, and dirty.
- Teachers sit in the back of the room marking papers or doing anything but paying attention to what is happening with their children.
- Teachers don't communicate plans to the artist.
- Teachers keep information to themselves that would help the artist work with children.
- Teachers talk negatively about children in the class *in front of* them.
- Teachers don't value the arts.

And then you read the articles by teachers praising the fabulous friendship that has blossomed between them and their collaborators and you know that as hard as a collaboration is, that is how rewarding such an enterprise is for the teacher, the artist, and of course the students.

A Parable

Once an artist named Artemis worked with a teacher in the classroom next door to Sandy, a fifth-grade teacher. One day Artemis went to Sandy in total despair. It seems Sandy's colleague wasn't giving the artist the time of day. As soon as Artemis would come in, the teacher would retreat with his papers to the back of the room. He would not assert his presence again until the bell rang for the end of the period. The artist asked Sandy whether, without getting the teacher in trouble, she could find out what was going on. She found a casual way to talk about the residency over lunch that day. "How's it going?" Sandy asked the teacher. With that her friend and neighbor really unloaded. He had not asked for an artist, did not want an artist, and he was damned if he was going to get involved in this residency. The principal was critical of the teacher because the kids were in the bottom half of the grade on reading tests, and then he sends an artist in who takes time away from preparing for the next test!

Sandy and the teacher talked the situation over and tried to find ways in which the artist could tap into the reading problem the kids were having. Because the artist was a painter, the tie-in with reading was not too obvious. They decided to have the kids illustrate their book reports in the hope that it would get them more involved in the content. (Most of the kids' book reports seemed to have been copied from the blurb on the jackets.) The artist had six lessons left, enough for a project of this type.

They called the artist and arranged for a special meeting. The artist came up with a wonderful idea: she would bring into class the mechanicals for book covers that she had prepared for different publishers. Then she and the teacher worked out a format to explain how editors choose the right cover for a novel. They then prepared a series of art lessons in which the students would illustrate their books from thumbnail sketch to finished mechanicals. The finished mechanicals were displayed in the front lobby as part of the school's reading program display, and everyone was happy! As a result of this experience, the kids learned their books on an entirely different level—considering symbolism, plot versus character, the importance of setting, and so on, as they determined what to show on the book's cover.

Planning for Content and Process

I always enjoy school reform planning sessions when knowledgeable arts advocates are part of the conversation. Instead of a narrow discussion regarding the reading or math standards, the talk inevitably turns to the notion of the many languages of learning and how all the standards can be addressed creatively. Recently, I was asked to join the planning committee of a midsized elementary school that was struggling to improve its students' academic performance by infusing the curriculum with arts experiences. Not a new idea, but new for this school. They started in the usual concrete way: they were committed to contracting with a museum and an organization of architectural designers to help them achieve school reform goals, and they needed to figure out what the kids should do. By using the word *do* as opposed to *learn* or *create*, they had already gotten themselves into trouble. The group found it easier to focus on one grade at a time (there were four classes per grade at this school). The second-grade teacher wanted the architect to "do something with the kids about China" because the teacher had spent the previous summer there and wanted to use what she had learned. The problem was that the required curriculum for the second grade was community, with the usual understanding that the community to be studied was the immediate community of this neighborhood school. The other teachers on the team were puzzled regarding how China would fit into their curriculum. After all, China was part of the sixth-grade curriculum.

As the architect responded to the problem, the teachers began to see an opportunity for comparing two communities as an extension of studying the local community. As the students began to identify the institutions that supported their local community (e.g., schools, houses of worship, local stores, firehouses, hospitals, community leaders), the architect began to show them how they could look at each of these aspects of a local contemporary Chinese community. They could find similarities and differences, they could see where structures represented the symbols that had meaning for the different communities, and so on. And the children could make objects that represented the two different communities. The comparative work could be done with three classes developing objects familiar to the local community and one class (with the teacher who had visited China) developing objects that were analogous but found in China. And so began the research process that eventually led to the creation of models representing the sites and buildings that could be described in terms of their use and meaning to the people living in those communities.

The more facile learners (the top class) did very well with the project. They could at the end describe what they had done, why, and tell elaborate narratives about their work and what they had learned from it. The children who needed more structured conversations, more background, and more help in making associations stumbled along as best they could. Their work was less appealing, overly general, with few ideas embedded into the structures they built. What had happened? Was this simply the continuation of how children learn and the inevitability of learning striation?

I think not. What had happened is what frequently happens when good ideas for classroom projects are not properly planned for the different kinds of learners sharing the same space. For all the propaganda about "cooperative learning," and "learning by discovery," there was not enough attention paid to how different youngsters were responding to the materials, the research approach, and the process of making associations. The children who were functioning at a lower level needed more time with knowledgeable adults. They needed time to talk through their work with the teacher, the architect, and any other adult (e.g., a student teacher) who happened to be assigned to the room. In pedagogical terms, they needed scaffolding. But that did not happen, and so the quick ones did well and the slower children did the best they could but without mastering much.

That in the proverbial nutshell is what happens when good ideas are unevenly implemented.

Curriculum Development for Elementary and Middle Schools

5

*W*e have all seen in the newspapers and on TV stories where children have found ways of expressing ideas and feelings in the arts, weaving facts and artifacts to demonstrate their mastery of various subjects or disciplines. Each story tends to tug at the heart and make the case that learning difficult material can be made more fun (and easier) if children are involved in the dramatic, musical, or visual arts or if they can make documentaries and animations to go along with textbook readings. Educators attend numerous local, state, and national conferences where projects are described showing how students learn history, math, science, and literature with great enthusiasm and accomplishment because the arts enliven the subject matter and make it real. While accepting the proposition that the arts help students learn the times table or a theory of light or sound, one needs to also examine the corollary to this proposition. That is, children and youth must also have command of the language of these arts domains if they are to find alternatives to traditional ways of demonstrating their understanding of the world and its complexities.

We know that each of the creative arts has its own language. In art the language is spoken through the arrangement of line, shape, form, texture color, and value; artists work with principles of balance, contrast, proportion, pattern, rhythm, emphasis, unity, and variety. In music the language is spoken through tone and rhythm, dynamics, melody, harmony, tempo, and timbre, with voice and other instruments creating patterns and compositions. In theatre the play is usually the thing, but the language is spoken through tone of voice, the use of body, and arrangement of objects in space. Dance has its own set of linguistic morphs, phrases, and gestures, each helping to communicate mood or meaning, action or thought. The point of mentioning the obvious is that children need to explore these languages just as they need to acquire, refine, and extend their spoken and written language. And they need to learn the languages by expressing ideas, feelings, and facts, just as they do in oral and written development. Their excursions into the languages of art need to be as reciprocal as reading is to writing, and speaking is to listening. Just as we do not expect children to learn to express themselves verbally by learning the rules of grammar first, we should not expect school-age children to first learn the elements and principles of an artistic discipline before experimenting with the discipline as a medium of ideas. In the current atmosphere of reform, how well do these ideas inform the process? Does high-stakes testing mitigate against the acquisition of expressive language?

Attempts have been made to look at what children are capable of doing, knowing, and understanding at various ages and stages of their development in the several arts domains. The information that such attempts have yielded should help those who use the arts to assist in improving education for children. But there needs to be an agent of support within the school to help the teachers adopt and align their teaching scenarios with their understanding of how children learn. Then teachers (and sometimes their students) need to figure out appropriate bridges between the arts domains and the other curricular areas where they expect to see more and better learning.

From Armenia's Center for Aesthetic Education to MoMA and Back

I learned this lesson well on two research excursions to Armenia in 1989 and 1990. Armenia was at that time an autonomous republic of the U.S.S.R., tucked away behind a corroding iron curtain. I was invited to study the Armenian way of teaching in and through the arts by Professor Pergrouhi Nazarian Svajian, an eminent cognitive psychologist whose family roots are deeply embedded in Armenia's tragic history. Armenia has a powerful artistic and intellectual tradition, which is conscientiously passed down to its preschoolers and nur-tured throughout primary and secondary school. The artistic work that students create is impressive and has attracted the attention of major universities and cultural institutions here and abroad. What could our American colleagues learn from this ancient culture?

When Pergrouhi and I met, she was the chair of the Secondary Education Department at Brooklyn College and I was her most recent hire, a lecturer in Secondary Art Education. We found that our philos-ophy of teaching meshed beautifully. As a cognitive psychologist she could underscore what I was doing intuitively with the validating the-ory of child development. As an art educator, I could provide exam-ples of how the theories of learning applied to the acquisition of visual language and graphic portrayal of meaning. We were a team.

Before our excursion to Armenia, Professor Svajian and I had col-laborated with the Museum of Modern Art (MoMA) in New York City on an early childhood program. We were both concerned that a model for preparing parents of young children to enjoy the art in museums was lacking, so we proposed one to MoMA, which, at that point, did not have such a program. In fact, their de facto education policy eliminated the museum as a site for young children. Their edu-cation programs were for high schoolers, college students, and adults. Children were not encouraged to visit, and when they did, they were not given any special orientation or support. Nonetheless, weary parents were sighted dragging their young charges from gallery to gallery in the parental hope that some good would result. We thought that there was a different way of introducing the museum to children.

At that time, I was advising a regional education unit on pro-grams for the gifted and talented.[1] I had access to parents, a budget for supporting training, and the connections with the museum. When I posed the project to the Museum's Education Director, Philip Yena-wine, he was enthusiastic and eager to learn a psychologically grounded, aesthetically oriented approach for teaching art to young children.

We designed a two-part experimental training program for par-ents of four- to seven-year-olds: Part One was a Thursday seminar for parents only, held after work from about 7 to 9 p.m. in the museum's new Education Center. Part Two was a Saturday morning session for

---

[1] The Board of Cooperative Education Services (BOCES) had hired me to direct their Gifted and Talented Programs after I had completed setting up the Westchester Arts Program, an extended-day/extended-week program at the local college (SUNY/Purchase College). I had a budget to subsidize the pilot as a way of developing offerings for parents of gifted and talented chil-dren. Because I believed that all children fit this category in one or more ways, all parents were eligible to participate in the pilot.

these same parents and their young children. For the pilot, we worked with about a dozen or so parents affiliated with Board of Cooperative Education Services (BOCES) schools in southern Westchester County. The parents had signed up for the pilot in response to an open invitation from BOCES to participate.

The Thursday evening session began with greetings by Phil Yenawine, and then Professor Svajian presented a mini-lecture on the developmental profile of children according to the prevailing cognitive theorists. She explained in the most comprehensible terms and anecdotes the theories of Piaget, Froebel, and Dewey and what they had to say about children and art. Parents responded enthusiastically, and they asked many questions. Then I talked about the ways adults can stimulate conversations with small children, including asking questions that require more than a "yes" or "no" answer, and that lead to speculation, putting one's self in the shoes of the painter, or the model, or the museum director, and learning how to take a picture apart and put it back together again verbally. Finally, Yenawine presented a short slide talk, having selected about a dozen paintings that are part of the museum's permanent collection and were available to see in the galleries. He selected paintings that told stories: Picasso's *Three Musicians*, Cezanne's *The Bather*, Van Gogh's *Starry Night,* and Matisse's *Dancers*, among others. He focused on pictures of familiar yet somewhat abstract scenes. He brought to each slide a knowledge of the artist and his intentions, flavoring his presentation with interesting anecdotes.

After discussing the slides, their special qualities, and the questions they stimulated, we gave each parent a packet of postcard reproductions of paintings that Yenawine had talked about (plus a few others) to take home and introduce to their children. Our idea was to set the stage for a "treasure hunt" on Saturday when the youngsters would try to find "their" pictures. Meanwhile, we asked parents to practice their conversational techniques and ask their children to pick from among the postcards the one they most wanted to see first.

Their homework paid off on the following Saturday when parents returned with children in tow for this very special occasion. No other visitors were allowed in the museum. We had it all to ourselves. We trooped upstairs after a quick orientation regarding what the morning would be like. The gates opening the galleries were still down; when all the children had assembled with their parents, the guard pushed a button and the gates to the first gallery rose. There was an audible gasp (just like in the theatre when the set stuns the audience) as the children saw the real pictures, so much larger and so much richer in color and texture. They searched out the paintings/postcards they had talked about with their parents. As we eavesdropped on various conversations between parent and child, we noted that both parents and children appeared relaxed and eagerly talked about what they saw. Some remarked on the size of the paintings (they were larger than anticipated), and some were surprised at how easy it was to make up a story about what they saw.

We had encouraged parents to ask questions such as "What do you think the three musicians were doing before they posed for the painting?" Or "Who do you think lived in the houses or sailed the boats or rode the horses?" "Why do you think the artist decided to paint the man's face red? Or blue? Or make the earth purple?"

When all the postcard pictures had been checked out, parents were encouraged to ask their children which pictures they liked the best. At the end of about forty-five minutes, we returned to the education center, where the parents met with Pergrouhi while I met with the children. The parents were delighted at how easy it was to engage their children in a conversation about a painting or about art in general. There had been no whining, no tugs of war, just an energetic quest for the paintings and animated conversations about what the children saw.

Meanwhile, the children sat in a circle with me on the floor and sorted out their postcards. They selected the one that represented the picture they most wanted to talk about. Each spent a few minutes describing the picture and, wherever possible, told a story that related the picture to the narrative. After each child had had a chance to participate, we joined the parents, who were debriefing in a separate section of the large room and celebrated the morning with apple cider and cookies.

The museum experience for small children was based on a firm understanding of what children from four to seven years old can grasp. The children (and their parents) had clear expectations of what was to occur at each stage of the experience. The gallery segment and the pre- and post-gallery conversations were timed to pass the wriggle test: not too short to be superficial and not too long to be tedious. The pilot program was deemed a success by all, and with some modifications that were made for financial reasons, the program continues to this day.

With this background of positive experience behind us, we were ready to develop new ideas that combined art learnings with psychological conditions. Pergrouhi was Vice President for Education of the Armenian General Benevolent Union (AGBU), an international network of individuals who support Armenians both in the Republic as well as in the Diaspora. The AGBU is one of the most prominent organizations that support the needs of Armenia and Armenians worldwide in health, economic development, and preservation of the intellectual as well as religious legacy of its people. In her many visits to Armenia, she had become very friendly with Henrik Igitian, who had founded and directed several Centers for Aesthetic Education where, during or after school, there were classes in the visual and performing arts. Pergrouhi had told me of the outstanding work that went on in these centers, despite meager budgets, limited facilities, and, more recently, an oil embargo. She wanted me to see what the Armenians were doing so we could share their practices with our American colleagues.

Despite war between Armenia and Azerbaijan, we flew off to Armenia in the dead of winter to see what the children were doing. We were accompanied by Lisa Garrison, a consultant to the Children's Museum of Manhattan (CMOM), one of the two sites where we had arranged to show a selection of children's work upon our return. Shortly after our plane landed, the airport was closed in response to the exigencies of war. We were welcomed with flowers and cheers, as if we were doing something heroic by being with them in their time of trouble. We did not feel like heroes, and were very touched by their warm greeting.

We spent most of our time in Yerevan, the capital of Armenia, where the first Center for Aesthetic Education was established in 1976 as part of the Education Ministry, and we traveled to some of the areas hardest hit by the previous year's horrendous earthquake. We found children aged four and five intently painting full scenes at their easels on nine-by-fourteen-inch paper using tempera or pastels. Every young artist worked with a full range of paint pots. They used scrap paper as palettes to mix colors. We observed classes of older children who painted subjects from observation (e.g., portraits, still lifes, neighborhood scenes) or from secondary experiences (e.g., folktales or home stories where they heard family members talk of war and earthquakes and other catastrophic threats to their being as well as celebrations and religious ceremonies). We noted that children worked on the same paintings for several sessions, putting the paintings away to "season" until they were ready to add, modify, or elaborate on a previous day's work. Part of their program at the centers included large doses of traditional tales relating to their religious heritage.

Ceramic work was prodigious, as was needle work, assisted by parents. Marionettes were made under the careful guidance of two marionette artists who have since moved to the United States. The entire teaching staff was composed of members of the artists union (of which Igitian was the head). They were all graduates of colleges of pedagogy. Despite an oil embargo that made it almost impossible to get around and required wearing coats and hats indoors for lack of heat, the centers were well attended by children whose parents sat in nearby anterooms, quietly chatting and drinking tea.

When we returned to the United States, we planned for an exhibition and a symposium to be held for teachers of art in the metropolitan New York area. Pergrouhi organized an Exhibition Committee with members of the AGBU; they got busy strategizing how this project could be best supported and disseminated to wider audiences. They raised money for a catalog as well as packages of greeting cards that could be sold at museum gift stores and by AGBU members. They also arranged for coverage by the Armenian press.

In the following spring, during one of the less warlike periods, I returned to Armenia, this time with my colleague, Professor Andrea Zakin of Lehman College's Art Education Department, and Charlie Wilson, my professional partner and husband. Our job was to look again at the teaching-learning process and to collect work for the exhibition. We looked even more carefully at the works-in-progress and the archives of paintings, drawings, sculptures, fabric designs, and other artifacts created over time by children enrolled at the Yerevan Center. On this trip we were entertained by a chorus of teenagers who were learning their parts for *Lullaby of Birdland*. We had a feeling that they did not understand what they were singing and, given the opportunity to confirm our hunch, we then were invited to teach the choristers about Charlie Byrd and why this song was really dedicated to him rather than the feathered species. The kids were relieved to find out that this was not about a bunch of birds up past their bedtime.

As Andrea and I traipsed through Yerevan's medieval stone village that housed many of the children's families, we also absorbed the fact that art was exhibited in all of the houses. Children grew up knowing not only who their ancestors were, but they also learned how their ancestors rendered the world as a real and mythological construct. (We had noticed the importance of art and music in the home on my first trip, where, even in the temporary boxcar housing for the earthquake victims, there were shelves of books, pianos, and pictures on the walls!)

We returned from Yerevan via Moscow, where we met with Igitian and made the final selections of work for the exhibition. Andrea directed the installation of the paintings and worked with CMOM staff to develop activities that would heighten visiting children's understanding of the paintings and the references within them. Our intention was to create a real gallery of work rather than a cutesy exhibition with buttons to push and knobs to twist. We wanted the children to relate to the art on its own terms with prompts from student docents. CMOM's director wanted a more interactive exhibition, so Andrea worked with the staff to ensure that the level of interactivity did not reduce the work to mere games and puzzles. When the exhibition traveled to the University of North Carolina (UNC), there was much more interaction with the work *qua* art, and children from the area were engaged in looking with prompts from a corps of trained student docents, in a program coordinated by the sponsor (The Blue Marble) and UNC teacher-fellows.

To launch the exhibition at CMOM, Howard Gardner, then co-director of Project Zero at Harvard's School of Education; Philip Jackson, head of the Curriculum Department at the University of Chicago; Judith Burton, from the Columbia University Teachers College; and Pergrouhi Svajian, now retired from Brooklyn College, shared their responses to the exhibit. They talked about children's art in general and the work in the exhibition in particular. Each noted the distinctive qualities of the work and contrasted the circumstances of creation in Yerevan with those in large American cities such as New York.

Pergrouhi and I wanted teachers and parents to see what children are capable of doing at various ages if the conditions for their creative work are in place. What were these conditions? The conditions are no easier to attain just because they are obvious, but here they are:

- Freedom for students to create and for pedagogues to search for new formulations of the traditional.
- Concern for the physical and spiritual development of each child at the Center.
- Emphasis on both mastery of techniques and individual expression.
- Pedagogic expertise—the teachers at the Center for Aesthetic Education are all fully trained master teachers, totally influenced by Igitian's vision of teaching.
- Artistic expertise—the teachers are all accomplished artists and members of the artists union of the U.S.S.R. Since the breakup of the Soviet Union, it is unknown whether the artists union continues to exist.
- Stimulating individuated assignments or problems to solve—the assignments are very often rooted in the world around them or in the icons that are dear to every Armenian family.

- Good materials—adult materials rather than crayons or other materials associated with traditional "children's art."
- Time and space to be a creative artist regardless of age—studio sessions may last for an hour or more. Children have the freedom to walk around and look at each other's work, and they can store a painting away for a while and come back to it at a later time.

As Pergrouhi wrote in the American General Benevolent Union report,

> Observations of children working at the Center reveal a philosophy in action. Spiritual and nationalistic values are almost palpable as youngsters of all ages struggle to master the language of art in its many dimensions. The children are, in fact, young storytellers whose artworks surmount national boundaries, ideologies, and petty differences. They provide a beacon of hope at a time when the world is in distress. (5)

As I review the material we developed during this Armenian period, it seems painfully appropriate because of the post-9/11 environment that we Americans live in. The nationalistic brand of work that marks Armenian children's visual and performing art is echoed in a lot of the artwork coming out of schools close to Ground Zero. Where the presence of American flags and exhortations to defend America were rare before 9/11, they abound in children's art now, as do the ghostly shapes of the World Trade Center twin towers.

It is important to note that the Armenian creative way progresses from concept or intention to form. The children participate in the conceptualization of their work with as much involvement as they do in the realization of the concept. "Then the two come together in the child's hand," explained Samuel Baghdassarian, one of the outstanding artist-teachers at the Center and a protégé of Igitian.

Responses to the Armenian children's art show at both CMOM and the University of North Carolina were enthusiastic. Teachers were struck by how sophisticated was the use of the elements of art by very young children. They were also struck by the way youngsters integrated folk history and nationalism into their work. But the Americans were skeptical about whether they could elicit similar responses from their students given the constraints under which they worked. For example, elementary art teachers generally work with classes of students for forty to forty-five minutes per week, give or take a holiday or two. They have little storage space, if any, so students have no place to put their work down for a while to gestate. Moreover, many art teachers are required to decorate the building with holiday-of-the-month drawings. These insipid *homages* to the calendar do nothing for the aesthetic sensibility of children but rather trivialize both art and the idea of celebration.

Art in Queens, New York

One does, however, see the occasional departures from the usual elementary school art, and it is striking how much can be done within ordinary constraints. I marvel still at the wonderful art program at PS 144 in Queens, New York. I was first introduced to the school when I agreed to evaluate their New York City Partners in Arts Education grant from the Center for Arts Education, an administrator of funds from the Annenberg Foundation and other funders. The school had hired, through the Queens Museum of Art, an unusually talented teaching artist, Aimée Mowrer, to launch a schoolwide art program that would complement a series of experiences at the museum. She started with a project that resulted in a gallery of self-portraits completed by every child in the school. The student cafeteria was transformed into a huge portrait gallery on the occasion of a reception for parents and dignitaries in honor of the school's receiving the four-year grant. The portraits were a confirmation of what young children at different stages of development can master with knowledgeable instruction.

Each portrait struggled to be an individual statement yet within certain conventions: the portraits were on the same size paper, but the paints and tools varied from grade to grade. As one gazed at the collection of kindergarteners through sixth graders, one could see the acquisition of modeling skills, the representation of light, the understanding of the physical head, the way that the facial features were created to express feelings. The gallery became an exposition of child development in visual language.

Later in the year, Aimée invited the children to the museum to study the landscapes of Charles Burchfield, a recognized early twentieth-century artist who had worked in Queens. When the fifth and sixth graders returned to school from their excursion, they took what they had seen as a model of what they might do. They toured their neighborhood with sketchpad in hand and later learned how to take a chosen sketch and work from it into a pastel landscape. The results were staggeringly mature as they integrated technical mastery with ideas they wanted to express about what they saw.

Aimée's students did not have to work within the forty-five minute limitation, however. She was able to meet her students twice a week for an hour or so in their classroom or in her art studio. She shared teaching responsibilities with the classroom teachers, who, in turn, used the occasion to heighten student understanding of the historical and geographical context of Burchfield (which addressed several standards of the social studies curriculum!). All of the work that Aimée accomplished was the result of careful planning between her and the classroom teachers, facilitated by the extraordinary Lois Olshan, PS 144's Annenberg grant coordinator and teacher of the school's gifted and talented program. Without the facilitation, the planning might not have been as meticulous; with Lois' availability to intervene when logistical or contextual problems occurred, Aimée was able to do her best work.

SARI: The Therapeutic Contribution of the Arts

Students need to use their various languages to say what is in their hearts and on their minds. Never was this point so poignantly made as in the aftermath of 9/11. I was asked to develop the School Arts Rescue Initiative (SARI) to help youngsters whose lives were directly affected by the tragedy to cope with the shattering experience of evacuation, loss of family and friends, and recognition that they could no longer take their safety for granted. Jack Rosenthal, president of The New York Times Company Foundation, for whom I serve as an advisor on arts education grants, asked me to put together a plan to get artists into the schools. We thought that if visual and performing artists could help youngsters create art, the results would be salutary both for the children and their teachers. We both understood that engaging in a creative process can at least take their minds off immediate concerns or, at best, help channel anxieties into a form that can be objectified and therefore provide a little relief.

We also knew that many of the arts organizations serving schools were heavily hit by the financial crunch that preceded 9/11 and the financial uncertainty that followed the attack. With SARI, we could give schools a chance to select an arts provider (a theatre, musical group, dance ensemble, gallery or museum, or teaching artist organization) from the Times Foundation's list of grantees and contract with it to provide an extended series of workshops in one or more arts forms. There were few restrictions other than that the workshops should enable kids to express ideas and feelings (theirs or someone else's). The workshops could be held during school, after school, or on the weekend, depending on the preference of the school's principal and planning committee. Almost $3 million in grant money in the form of arts credits (similar to vouchers) were spent by schools over a three-year period, with the result that students could have their say about such far-reaching topics as loss, conflict, intergroup communication, the importance of friendship, and national values. In original plays performed as works-in-progress or polished presentations, in paintings and drawings exhibited in schools and their immediate community, in sculptures installed as public memorials, and in choral and instrumental concerts and classroom improvisations, students found their voices and their comfort in the creative arts. And in the process of developing SARI, funders and schools found that it did not take a forest worth of paper to define clearly what they wanted to do with the students and how the arts programming would transpire. SARI also encouraged artists to work with concepts before technical issues so that, as they do in Armenia, the two could be fused ultimately through the child's virtual hand.

Many of the schools that participated in SARI from Long Island, New York, and suburban New Jersey found the SARI program a jumpstart for developing new approaches to learning. In Hoboken and Weehawken, the use of arts organizations as partners in learning was a relatively new phenomenon that has become a continuing feature of the schools. The impact of the program on disaffected students has been considerable, because they found in the arts programs a safe and supportive relief from the other parts of their school day.

Reggio Emilia as a Model of Early Childhood Education

Another great influence on my understanding of what children are capable of creating, given the appropriate context in which to create, was Loris Malaguzzi, founder of the Reggio Emilia approach to early childhood education. Malaguzzi, like the seminal educational figures who preceded him, was an intuitive teacher who was also a born organizer and leader. His pedagogical and psychological training in Italy polished his approach, but in the tradition of Froebel, Montessori, and Dewey, his actions preceded his theoretical structure. In the U.S., Reggio became the flavor of the month in the early 1990s as word about the extraordinary early childhood work spread through a television program featuring it as part of a series on creativity. A replication of Reggio originated at the Children's Capitol Museum in Washington, D.C., founded and directed in its first several years by Ann Lewis. Sadly, the model closed in 1995, but that excellent school influenced my decision to secure a magnet grant to help create the Barnard Early Childhood Center in New Rochelle, New York. Barnard had been a de facto racially isolated school, ignored by its upper middle class neighborhood families, who opted to send their children any where but there. Within two years after receiving the grant, the school had attracted a racially and economically diverse population with a long waiting list. The Department of Education's Magnet Schools Assistance Program enabled the Barnard School staff to be trained and coached by Ann Lewin and her associates for two years. Barnard's teachers and parents not only created a Reggio-like pre-K and kindergarten, but also expanded and adapted the concept through the second grade. The essential ingredients of Reggio have been maintained: close observation of children, record keeping of progress through portfolio analysis, incorporation of parents into all aspects of schooling, establishing aesthetically sensitive classrooms suitable for small children by elimination of visual static and all commercial bulletin board kitsch, employment of an *atelierista* or arts specialist, extensive involvement of parents in the operations of the school, and use of external sites and resources as part of the educational mix. The Barnard model serves as a lesson in model making and preservation of islands of excellence. One of the fine outcomes of the Reggio model is that students in the program, drawn from a lottery, continue to do well when they move on to the third grade in other New Rochelle schools. According to assistant superintendent, Jeff Korostoff, the Reggio students consistently score in the upper brackets on standardized tests.

Developing Substantive Curriculum

Many arts-centered schools have an ambitious program of writing new curriculum guides and manifestos. This is mostly because they get grants that require written curriculum as part of the deliverables. Many of the documents, including those put on the Net, are far from exemplary. Most, in fact, seem either unimaginative or overambitious, leading to frustration for learners and teachers who try to implement them.

The presence of juried and unjuried curriculum writing efforts on the Internet gives teachers at least a starting point as they search for appropriate content and methods to teach through the arts. What the teachers need, however, are templates they can use to assess the quality of curriculum units and lessons that are posted. Such templates need to be based on the best practices outlined as follows and distilled from several outstanding writers on the subject (Heidi Hayes-Jacobs, Bob Marzano, Elliot Eisner, Arthur Ellis, and Caro Stuen, etc.) and my own observations:

Figure 5–1   A Template for Developing Curriculum: Learning in and/or Through the Arts

1. *The theme.* The theme must be generative, suggesting many paths of inquiry that will lead to a full discussion of topics embedded in the theme. It is best to state a theme as a problem with many alternative solutions. An example of a good theme is "Can we protect our forests without sacrificing our current way of life?" It begs for research of the past and present situation of forests; it suggests many subtopics, including how artists have portrayed forests over the centuries; it also suggests representation of information in many graphical forms; it also suggests the use of music that uses the forest as an inspiration; and it requires daily reading of newspapers for articles relating to the forest and forest-related businesses, including lumbering, paper manufacturing, and animal protection. It also suggests a set of culminating projects, including a panel presentation of responses to the thematic question with built-in role-plays for spokespersons with particular points of view. Finally, it encourages students to contemplate the future—so necessary if we are to develop informed, civic-minded citizens.

2. *Goals and objectives for students to achieve.* The curriculum unit should specify what knowledge and skills and at what levels of proficiency students will be required to learn. In the forest unit, such goals could include an understanding of the complexity of the problem and implications of various political, economic, and ecologic policies. Objectives would include enabling students to read and interpret information related to the forest in books (cite specific titles), magazines (cite specific titles), and newspapers. Students would also be taught how to compose a forest scene either from photographs or reproductions or on-site sketching and painting of forest scenes, and interpret the works to others. They might be asked to record and identify distinctive forest sounds (particularly if they live near a forest). Students could learn how to arrange sounds into a musical composition (after studying the work of composers such as Elizabeth Swados).

continues

Figure 5–1 continued

3. *Activities and outcomes.* This section would describe a range of activities that students (some, most, all) might engage in while participating in this unit. Activities should be listed complete with references and anticipated outcomes. There should be research activities, activities that require placing the students in critical situations (role-plays) that require resolution (e.g., tree huggers versus lumberjacks, senators versus lobbyists, etc.), and activities that require students to prepare essays with a distinct point of view. Additional activities might include reading certain key literary works such as Longfellow's *Evangeline* or one of Thoreau's sections from *Walden* or one of John McPhee's essays from *The New Yorker* on the forest.

4. *Assessment of learning and instruction.* Tests, quizzes, and rubrics to evaluate artistic projects plus methods of interpreting results should be included in this section. This is usually the weakest part of most published units because the writers do not include actual tests or rubrics. Curriculum templates should include a way to rate this section for its usefulness by the average teacher. Just saying tests and rubrics should be used will not do!

5. *Teacher talk.* Whenever I construct curriculum units, I always include a section where I virtually talk with a teacher who plans to use the unit. It will include caveats, discussion of the supplies and materials that will be needed to complete the unit, and suggestions regarding how the teacher can manage the many facets of the unit in whole class, partial class, and individual assignments. There is usually a discussion of how to protect the integrity of the artistic efforts so they do not appear to be merely token but are substantive contributions to the anticipated learnings.

Disseminating Unit Plans

Now that it is possible to burn CDs with illustrations of student projects, the unit may be disseminated as a work-in-progress so that students and teachers can contribute to each of the categories. Live action, tapes, and stills, can all be incorporated onto a CD for dissemination to others through websites, emails, and other as-yet-unanticipated means.

6 Curriculum Development for High Schools

*M*y earliest effort to use the arts to help the school reform process was related to how schools could make the best use of teaching artists. High schools tended to be more resistant to the notion that artists could enhance teaching programs or contribute to the attainment of academic goals. Moreover, high schools tended to have a full or at least partial complement of art and music teachers, and the English departments tended to take care of drama. When it came to dance, some schools had active dance clubs run on an extracurricular basis, but the number of curricular dance programs was almost too small to count. This situation has changed in the last decade, primarily because of two factors: (a) the availability of money from tax levy budgets or special funds for high schools as well as elementary and intermediate schools, and (b) the introduction of various funded partnerships: (1) Arts in the Basic Curriculum (ABC), South Carolina; (2) Arts for Academic Achievement: Minneapolis Annenberg Challenge for Arts Education; (3) the New York City Partnership for Arts Education administered by the Center for Arts Education; (4) the A+ Schools Program based now at the University of North Carolina in Greensboro; (5) Transforming Education Through the Arts Challenge (TETAC), a multicity partnership; and (6) the Chicago Arts Partnerships in Education

(CAPE). While some of these projects did not include high schools, they encrouaged students and parents to advocate for stronger high school art programs. In the process of funding high schools, some excellent programs gained attention and have become models for other schools to emulate.

One of the first high school drama in education programs I was asked to evaluate was a partnership between the American Place Theatre (APT) and the High School of Humanities in Manhattan called Urban Writes (a pun that I am still not sure that the students understood). The Urban Writes program revealed the strengths and weaknesses generic to partnerships between arts organizations and high schools and it also demonstrated where the curriculum is most hospitable to artistic infusion. How Urban Writes dealt with the inevitable problems and challenges associated with working within an urban high school is instructive to teaching artists, arts organizations, and secondary school educators.

Urban Writes was the brainchild of the creative team at APT. APT approached Humanities High School to cooperate in a proposal to the National Endowment for the Arts (NEA), and their efforts were rewarded by a three-year grant to establish a model arts education program and prove its effectiveness. APT had invited Humanities High School to participate based on the principal's enthusiastic response to another of APT's programs, Literature (or "Lit") to Life. Lit to Life is a very artful program that involves the production of one-actor plays based on novels that were on the high school reading list. Wynn Handman, co-founder of APT and a nationally recognized mentor and coach to some of Broadway's finest actors and playwrights, did most of the early adaptations, and he has helped other writers to craft additional plays for APT's now considerable repertoire.

As anyone in the grants world knows, most proposals require a detailed evaluation plan, and many call for an external evaluator. When I was asked to consider joining the APT–Humanities High School project team as evaluator, I was pleased to accept. During the course of the partnership, Susannah Halston, general manager of APT, and Russell Granet, APT education director, worked hard to get the initial phase of the three-year program up and running despite the usual problems one confronts in working with schools. Teachers needed to be oriented to the program, its goals, and activities. Students needed to be placed in the elective classes where Urban Writes would be taught. The English department chair had to get on board because she had not been in place when the proposal was written. Human relationships had to be established between the artists and their partner teachers. And everyone had to get to know the targeted students, who had varying writing and acting abilities and different patterns of attendance.

Russell came aboard after the proposal was funded and had the unenviable task of hopping on the proverbial moving train since the originator of the program, Tracy Hirsch, left her job at APT to move to Hawaii. A quick learner and fresh from work with New York University's Creative Arts Team, Russell was able to make the program his own by the end of the year. But the process was extremely taxing: every solution seemed to generate new problems whether logistical, academic, or interpersonal. Rehearsal space, substitute teachers, unexpected conflicts in schedule, misunderstandings, and pressures related to the end-of-year Regents exams all plagued Russell's path. Most of the problems that Russell and the Urban Writes artists and teachers encountered occurred in the first year when no one had a really clear picture in mind of where all of the work would lead the classes. The second and third years were markedly different because everyone benefited from the first year's lessons.

For the artists involved (actors, playwrights, directors), the opportunity to work with older students was very attractive. The artists were themselves quite young and could relate to the hip-hop generation and teenage humor easily. They felt comfortable talking with the majority of students, but they had more difficulty with the small but volatile disaffected students in this difficult high school. They could not come into class and expect that homework assigned during the previous session would be completed and ready to work from. Artists mistakenly relied on teachers to follow through with assignments between Urban Writes workshops and were frequently disappointed with the results. Managing the classroom in the beginning was problematic, and keeping small groups of students working well and independently was particularly difficult, especially in those cases where the teacher was not invested.

The High School of the Humanities was a large city high school with a special curricular focus on the humanities that had replaced a failing comprehensive high school. The school was founded after a protracted battle with the Board of Education to create a high school that placed special value in a strong humanities curriculum. The school is physically imposing but rather depressing with its wide dark corridors, dingy-looking classrooms, and omnipresent security personnel. In the original plan for the school, the English, history, and arts departments were supposed to be strengthened, and students would have opportunities to fill their programs with humanities electives.

The multicultural student body (approximately sixteen hundred students) is largely drawn from the southern half of Manhattan. Ethnically, it is approximately 22 percent white (mostly Eastern European immigrants), 20 percent African American, 30 percent Hispanic, and 30 percent Asian.[1] Humanities High School is typical of many high schools in Manhattan. It is well served by corporate and cultural institutions based in New York. NBC, for example, helped the school reconstruct its auditorium, which now has state-of-the-art technology to enhance student performances. The Manhattan Theatre Club and Pearl Theatre Company have provided theatre education programs for selected classes, as has New York University and some eight or nine other arts organizations. Despite this surfeit of partnerships, the school has a rather dismal performance record. There is a dramatic drop out rate between the eleventh and twelfth grades. Only about 45 percent of its eleventh graders pass the Regents or Alternative Examinations in Reading, Writing, and Mathematics. A small school-within-the-school provides a nontraditional college prep program, although students in the general education program may take college prep courses as well.

Midway through the period when I was evaluating the program, a new principal was hired to replace the principal who had originally signed on to the program. This made it difficult for APT because the new principal was more concerned about raising the math and science scores than boosting the importance of the arts and humanities. (This tendency to put principals in charge of high schools without regard to their expertise or passion continues to amaze.) To the new principal's credit, the school tone began to improve under her leadership, and while initially disengaged from the program, she did become more enthusiastic after she saw its effect on students during the culminating experience.

My role as external evaluator was to see how this original and ambitious program would unfold and what, if any, positive effects could be detected in student performance. I needed to examine the hypotheses underscoring the purpose of the partnership. What if, the APT staff wondered, we work with Humanities students over a longer period of time than with Lit to Life, merging our expertise as playwrights and actors with the pedagogical and curriculum-centered expertise of selected English teachers? Would students develop a greater appreciation of live theatre? Would students find in themselves talents they did not know they had? Would students find affirmation of their lived lives through the creation of original theatre?

Other questions emerged during the course of the three-year venture focusing on the institutional partnership between a high school

---

[1] Source: NYC Annual School Report, 1996–1997.

and a producing theatre. What would happen if the theatre became a regular, reliable feature of the English curriculum? How would the school respond to the continuous presence of outsiders? What if the personnel who signed on in the first year changed from year to year? How would one establish continuity of program in a school where classes were organized by semester rather than by year? How could the ambitious goals of a partnership be achieved given the way schools are organized?[2] How could a program sustain its credibility and work with a high school without endangering the creative process? And how could the program sustain a level of excellence when theatre personnel and school personnel changed in midstream?

Over the three years of Urban Writes, some answers to these thorny questions began to emerge, which may suggest some general bits of wisdom for practitioners of theatre education within a high school context.

Description of the Program

For three years, the High School of the Humanities offered an English elective called, understandably, Urban Writes, taught by teachers from the English department in partnership with artists associated with APT.[3] The course featured novels that embraced themes and settings that were analogous to situations in which teens frequently find themselves.[4]

Joseph Edward, playwright and actor; Candido Tirado, playwright; Eileen P. O'Connell, actor/educator; Rinne Groff, actor/director; Liz Stanton, stage manager; and Helen White, independent consultant who is a director and specialist in youth theatre, constituted the artis-

---

[2] Forty-minute periods of instruction, regular interruptions of the instructional schedule, constant interruptions via the public address system, multiple programs competing for the same young people's involvement, to say nothing of the domination of high-stakes testing over everything happening within the building were just the typical kinds of constraints.

[3] This is an unusual way of partnering. Rarely does an arts education organization remain in residency for full academic semesters, and even more rarely is an elective class created around a partnership. There is a lesson here for arts-centered schools, particularly, but also for any high school partnership that aspires to make a long-term impact on students.

[4] I always felt that they missed an opportunity to help students transform scenes from novels that they were reading into dialog and stage directions. Had they done this, they could have grappled with the inner meanings of certain passages and made decisions regarding how selected scenes could be played out. They also could have emulated techniques that Wynn Handman used in doing the "real" play at APT for Lit to Life.

tic staff that worked directly with students and Humanities teachers. Patricia Adler, English department chair, and Judy Tucker, Special Education department chair, provided the school administrative support; Wanda Caine, Dr. Maryam Habibian, and Cynthia A. Olphie were the core participating English teachers. Other teachers participated in the project in the first and second year, but the teachers who stayed for the entire life of the project were the three just mentioned. Teachers participated on a voluntary basis and could involve more than one of their classes if they wished to do so and if the budget permitted.

Elements of Urban Writes

By the third year of the program, the partnership had generated program elements that ultimately accounted for its success:

- *Two planning retreats per year that involved all of the participating APT administrators and artists and Humanities administrators and teachers.* The retreats were used to make sure that everyone was on the same page regarding the year's plan. Schedules would be examined to ensure that testing days, vacations, and other interruptions were accounted for. After the first year, retreats were used to review the previous year's work and develop a schedule and action plan semester by semester. This was the time when participants could modify the previous year's program by making the kinds of adjustments that were recommended in the previous year's evaluation report.
- *Orientation of participating students to goals and objectives of Urban Writes at APT by APT staff.* Students got an opportunity to interact with Wynn Handman and get the feel of a real theatre. APT used this occasion to make sure students heard about the program directly from the arts partner rather than as interpreted by the participating teachers. This strategy attempted to preclude misunderstandings that occur when a third party describes a process that the first or second party has invented.
- *Introduction of a distinct playwright sequence in partnership with a working playwright (Candido Tirado) and partner English teachers.* Students began to experiment with dialog and plot conventions introduced by Tirado and received detailed feedback after each exercise was completed.
- *Lit to Life presentations.* Students attended three plays at the APT space. They asked questions of both the actor and the playwright.

Over time, their questions became more sophisticated, a result of their having wrestled with the creation of dialog from narrative. During the final year, the three performances were based on the following novels: *Dreaming in Cuban* by Christina Garcia; *Black Boy* by Richard Wright, and *The Glass Menagerie* by Tennessee Williams. In prior years, *The House on Mango Street* by Sandra Cisneros, Richard Wright's *Black Boy,* and *The Kitchen God's Wife* by Amy Tan were seen, as well as *Down These Mean Streets* by Piri Thomas and *Manchild in the Promised Land* by Claude Brown. *Manchild* has become one of APT's signature works as performed by Joseph Edward.

- *Informal class-to-class presentations of works-in-progress.* Playwright Candido Tirado and APT actors performed scenes written by Humanities students so they could see what happens when their words are spoken by professional actors. The experience helped motivate the kids to continue their work and to respect the creative process and its rewards.
- *Director's workshops for teaching artists and teachers led by Helen White.* With one exception, the English teachers had no experience as writers or performers. In order for them to understand what was being demanded of their students, it was essential that they go through many of the exercises that artists would be assigning to students. Teachers needed to understand emotionally how difficult the work was, how it can often lead to self-conscious giggling, and how they too could find the artist in themselves.
- *Improvisations (in small groups) and written scene development led by teaching artists.* Improvisations not only help student writers find the voices of their characters, but they also help overcome the first resistance to play writing as forced writing. Improvs put the fun into the project from the beginning.
- *Scene refinement.* The editing, polishing, and pruning process helps students to see that the first draft is just that—a first attempt.
- Preparation for production at Humanities (rehearsals, script revisions, design backdrop)
- Dress Rehearsals for performance at APT
- Performance on APT's professional mainstage
- Reflection on program in its entirety by entire cast and evaluator in an effort to get students to understand the various dimensions of what they had experienced

The students were an inquisitive, energetic group who, after a period of uncertainty about what Urban Writes was about and what they were going to have to do, enthusiastically embraced the activities and the artists. Some had volunteered for the program; others were "volunteered." Some were familiar with live theatre; others had never been exposed to live performances of nonmusical theatre. (New York has dozens of opportunities for students to attend live performances during the school day or in the evening thanks to the educational programs of various nonprofit and commercial theaters and the Theatre Development Fund. Teachers and students generally opt for the musicals, however, for class trips.)

One of the first techniques we used to ascertain the achievement of students was a review of their Regents portfolios, substitutes for a standardized English exam that is traditionally used as an exit credential for a high school diploma. As a former high school English teacher, I was dismayed by a random sample of portfolios. Their writing was weak to the extreme. Their essays were superficial stabs at writing. Not only was their paragraph and sentence structure weak, but most of them also lacked any style. Metaphorical writing was rarely evident. The use of a simple three-part format—introduction, development, conclusion—was rarely observed. Most disappointing was that the grades on these portfolios were much too generous. Since the completion of the first year of the program, greater attention has been paid to writing in English classes.

Supervisory Support

The APT program was housed within the English department, whose leadership also changed during the course of the three-year program. The supervisor of the English department left after the first year and was replaced for the remaining two years of the program by an acting interim chair, Patricia Adler. Pat's enthusiasm for the program grew from skeptical to enthusiastic supporter as she saw how the students were stimulated to read more and work harder in general. Time will tell whether she can make an impact on the quality of writing evidenced in the portfolios.

Many lessons were learned as this innovative program evolved— lessons that should be useful to those arts organizations and schools that are considering adopting the model in the future. Many of the lessons detailed in the following sections have to do with dealing with the inevitable aspects of working with a shifting population within the typical urban high school.

PERSONNEL CHANGES

Any multiyear program is likely to encounter changes in personnel. The question for the project director is how to prepare for these changes and, once made, how to protect the integrity of the program while adjusting to new personalities. In Urban Writes, the changes occurred within both organizations. The school changes turned out to be felicitous. The final cohort of teachers was the strongest of them all. All three were highly motivated and eager to put into effect the program elements available to them. Their work in helping to shape students' contributions was invaluable. The final artistic team was also the smoothest of the teams formed over the three years. Although they only worked together for one semester, they quickly worked out a complementary relationship that enriched the program. One factor that may account for this was that Helen White, the project consultant, knew more precisely what to look for when she replaced one of the artists. Another factor may have been Russell Granet's newly acquired comfort with his own role as not only facilitator but leader of the project. Granet initiated several small but important adjustments during the third year that helped create a positive context for the work. Liz Stanton, part of the APT Education Department team, made substantial contributions to the program as stage manager for the final production. She was able to stimulate the actors to acquire more theatrical use of the stage space and worked cooperatively with White and the actors.

COMPLEXITY OF THE PROGRAM

Funded programs are frequently marked by their complexity if only to please prospective funders with their imaginative approach to a partnership. Applicants are encouraged to take on a variety of challenges through a variety of means. This often results in unwieldy programs with multiple elements that are difficult to control. Program complexity, however, requires versatile management. In this instance, the capacity of management grew as the project coordinator's skills increased. It was not until the third year of this program that *meaningful* planning between artists and teachers occurred. Before that, the planning was mostly a show-and-tell: artists explained what they were prepared to do, the teachers assented, scheduling conflicts were considered, and the work commenced. By the third year, planning became more substantive and responded to perceived problems encountered in previous years. Teachers, students, and artists explored underlying themes in the selected literature and discovered how to make those themes translate meaningfully into adolescent concerns. And they planned ways to make the themes dramatically feasible. It took time for the participants to deal with the complexities of the program. When they recognized how important it was not just to share, but also to plan collaboratively, the program became a more powerful experience for all.

Understanding the School as Its Own Culture

It is commonplace to say that schools are unique, often reflecting the strengths and weaknesses of their leaders. High schools are particularly unique; they are buildings that are like micro-cities, filled with politics, issues of governance, and petty jealousies that can make or break innovative programs. For an outside organization to flourish in a partnership with a school, it is mandatory that the outsider understand and, to the extent it can, work within the customs of the culture. This, of course, makes it difficult to act as a change agent, which conflicts with some of the rationale for partnerships. Part of understanding and working within another's culture is figuring out how to get people to commit and fulfill promises. For example, the Year Two teachers committed themselves to developing an Urban Writes curriculum guide that would interface with the Urban Writes residencies provided by APT. Such a curriculum writing project was to be underwritten by the school with its discretionary funds. Neither teacher fulfilled her obligations regarding that project. And with the change of principals, it appeared that school funds might not be used to pay for the work, as previously promised. The lack of a teacher–artist developed joint curriculum that outlined all learning activities and assessment practices limited the deeper impact that Urban Writes might have had on many of its students.

Common Goals and Standards of Excellence

One of the missing links in Urban Writes was a description of what could and should be expected of students by the end of the third year in language that everyone could understand. Because the teachers' commitment to write an Urban Writes curriculum during the summer between years two and three was abrogated, there was no common document to refer to as students developed their scenes. In the meantime, the English department's portfolio review process did not yield the kind of writing that would help define the impact of Urban Writes on student literacy. The Humanities portfolio review process did not include a highly developed set of standards for acceptable and exceptionally good work. Consequently, the students had no clear statement of expectations toward which they could aim. The lack of such articulation may explain why most of the written work by Urban Writes students was so disappointing initially.

Putting Theatre Arts to Work

School deficits notwithstanding, APT dealt with these conditions in an exemplary way. Each year they found new ways to deal with the crises of the previous year. They extended the amount of time spent in the school and the number of sessions held with the students. They began each year with a full-day planning retreat and brought the participating adults together for midyear assessment and planning. They involved Helen White within a more clearly defined context. They tried to communicate more effectively with each other and with the larger staff at Humanities. Ultimately, they accepted the limitations set by the school and tried to work within them. Consequently, in the third year of this program they produced an educational and theatrical hit.

When playwright Candido Tirado joined the artistic team, the young people got a taste of what it was like for a professional to develop a play and clearly profited from having a professional playwright guide them through the thinking and writing process. Tirado's work showed in the more genuine voices that emerged in the final year's production. He encouraged on-your-feet exercises that engaged even the shyest and least motivated students. By the end of the semester, most of the students had written scenes containing well-defined characters in some kind of conflict. A corps of APT trained professional actors took the most developed scenes and presented a staged reading to the delight of the classes and their teachers. Students beamed as the theatre of their imagination was realized on the stage. It was truly a magical moment, and it established a firm foundation for the hard work to be accomplished during the spring semester. Another element that helped strengthen the program was the introduction of professional actors at midyear. By reading the scenes that students created, they showed how much actors contribute to the dynamics of a script. The students' work affirmed the idea that they could write imaginatively and integrate what they heard and observed in their daily lives.

In May, each class presented its series of scenes before their fellow students in a special assembly program and, following some further direction and polishing, the production moved to the APT for an audience of parents and friends. Some students, having participated in Urban Writes the previous year, were prepared for the effect of the experience. For most, however, seeing their work performed by fellow students was not just cool; it was a character-forming event.

One of the finer aspects of the program was the exemplary way artists with different ethnic or racial identities worked together. Students caught a glimpse of how to work across arbitrary boundaries in order to deliver an artistic product of quality. The experience helped foster improved relationships in other classes that APT students attended.

The prospects for school reform through this partnership, however, were never realized. Neither the principal nor the department chair paid much attention to the program until the culminating performance at APT. Teachers would have been hard put to find out about it if they were not participants. This was particularly unfortunate because several opportunities were made available to the school to highlight the program as a successful way to motivate low-performing students and to encourage them to broaden their world. While the usual lip service was paid at appropriate moments, Urban Writes was usually treated as marginal to the school's daily life, despite the regularity of APT services over the three school years.

Tentative Answers

How did working over a longer period of time, combining the expertise of playwrights and actors with the expertise of selected English teachers in curriculum and pedagogy affect student attitudes toward the theatre? Would students develop a greater appreciation of live theatre? Interviews with students during and after the final performance indicated that most recognized the value of live theatre and now actually loved nonmusical theatre as a genre. They attended on their own time several off-Broadway and Broadway plays including Joseph Edward's play, *Fly,* produced by APT during the residency. They visibly thrilled to the performance of *The Glass Menagerie,* another APT production, and demonstrated a level of understanding that even evaded some critics when Tennessee Williams' play was first produced.

Would students find in themselves talents that they did not know they had? Yes. Each class yielded evidence that students who thought they had no talent found that their written work or acting had a power that evoked admiration from their teachers and peers. More than a few described the work of their classmates in admiring tones.

Would students find affirmation of their lived lives through the creation of original theatre? The scenes that were presented as the culmination of Urban Writes convincingly showed an adolescent's view of adult and teenage behavior. Students discovered they did not have to create faux monster movies or soap operas as they did the first year; they could find real dramatic and comedic sources in their own situations. They could poke fun at real-life situations or move an audience by depicting some of the agonies of growing up in a world infected by AIDS and teenage pregnancy. The quality of the third year's work was as much a function of the ability of the staff to work more effectively as it was from student effort. Students would not have been able to put forth and sustain their efforts without the skillful sessions and feedback from the APT artistic staff.

What would happen if theatre became a regular, reliable feature of the English curriculum? In most New York City high schools, theatre is a regular part of the curriculum within the English department. High school English departments have partnerships (contracts) with theatre organizations, varying from year to year. Although theatre is a legitimate part of the curriculum, it is not available to all students. As for Urban Writes, it is an expensive program and not easily reproduced within a regular school budget. Like so many ambitious projects of this kind, unless there is a generous underwriter, the project will not remain within the school's regular offerings.

How would the school respond to the continuous presence of outsiders? Teachers and students not involved with the program hardly noticed the APT staff. One of the teachers with a theatre education background was not particularly hospitable to the program at first. This is not an unusual situation and is similar to the reaction of some art teachers to visual arts teaching artists. Although the teachers have the steady salary and the benefits, they don't have the glamour that the teaching artists bring with them. Oddly enough, the teaching artists get a little depressed when they see how hard they work and how much less money they earn and how little in the way of benefits they have.

What if the personnel who signed on in the first year changed from year to year? It actually helped the program develop! Each year the program made a fresh start, given the many changes in personnel involved. What helped, of course, was the continuous presence of

Susannah Halson and Russell Granet, APT's general manager and education director, respectively. They kept the ship on course and brought it into safe harbor.

How would one establish continuity of program in a school where classes were organized by semester rather than by year? Continuity of experiences across semesters is very difficult to obtain. Students have individually designed programs in most high schools and are not easily assigned to preferred classes without losing some other class assignment they need or want. Nonetheless, Humanities High School programmers tried their best to put as many students from the first semester into second semester Urban Writes classes. My own feeling is that they should just offer the elective class in one semester and conclude the semester with a performance or staged readings and not try to work against existing program constraints.

How could the ambitious goals of a partnership be achieved, given school constraints that worked against the creative process (forty-minute periods of instruction, regular interruptions of the instructional schedule, multiple programs competing for the same young people's involvement)? The commitment of participating artists and teachers helped overcome the barriers and constraints presented by this typical large urban high school. By the third year, there was a more solid relationship between the two institutions. At the end of the third year and the end of the funding cycle, there was an indication that, because of the glowing response to the third year of this program, a genuine partnership could develop. At this writing, the partnership, ever evolving, is still in place at the high school.

At the end of the grant period, it was helpful to reflect on the dimensions and complexity of this project. Each dimension required a set of expectations distinct from the others. For example, when considering the quality of the program, I looked for evidence of artistic achievement emerging from student efforts at creative work. I looked for genuine voice in the original scenes, as well as an understanding of the demands of good writing and convincing acting. I looked for evidence that the students could evoke humor and sympathy, empathy and distrust as they created their scenes. And I looked for students who thrived while working within the demands of theatre.

When considering the complexity of the work, I looked for the artistic and intellectual challenge placed before the students. Most theatre partnerships ask artists and teachers to provide a context for shared creative work despite a limited number of teaching sessions and rehearsals. They ask students and teachers to deal with a myriad of new situations: writing scenes, responding critically to performed works, balancing other teaching and artistic obligations with teaching and learning. They usually ask their artists to make themselves at home in a foreign culture and work collaboratively with people drawn from entirely different backgrounds who speak the language of pedagogy, not art.

Urban Writes delivered on dimensionality and complexity. It enabled young people to find their voices and produce creative work of quality. And it provided a challenge that forced students to look beyond the conventions of popular culture to examples set by attending several of the productions generated by APT. Urban Writes did not produce campfire skits; it produced small plays that were microcosmic displays of what high schoolers understand. Urban Writes was a serious effort to unite disengaged students with the larger cultural scene of New York through regular involvement with APT. And it worked, despite some peripheral distractions encountered when the two cultures of theatre and school clashed.

Was it worth it? By the end, despite some earlier reservations, everyone involved with the program was convinced of its value. The students' work as actors, playwrights, and stagehands was excellent. The involvement of Special Education students was particularly heartening. No one in the audience could tell who the Special Ed students were, nor did they care. Students performed long monologues, witty scenes that required professional timing, and ensemble footwork that required intense concentration. The plot lines and characterizations were more complex than in previous years; the ensemble work was truly together. Teachers gained a new appreciation for what their students could accomplish given the opportunity to learn and demonstrate achievement.

Cooperation between artists and teachers was exemplary by the third year and both groups benefited from working with each other. The performance at APT (a refinement of a performance of scenes at Humanities) demonstrated how the team transformed rather disjointed staging into sophisticated, unified scenes. Students, teachers, and artists were justifiably proud of their work.

APT learned about public high schools in New York City in ways that it could never have discovered from its more traditional programs. Moreover, it found a niche for itself as a coach to teachers as the latter attempted to use theatre techniques in making their curriculum come alive. APT discovered how important clear goals and objectives are when delivering a program to a high school. APT had worked in Humanities High School previous to the Arts Plus project, but the program was not very complex: students were invited to the theatre to see their required literature transformed into compelling theatre pieces. The students and actors talked about the work and found meanings in the novels that otherwise would have remained hidden. This taste of collaboration became the foundation for exploring a deeper, more complex partnership.

As a result of the Arts Plus partnership, the school established an Urban Writes course within the curriculum, and is committed to finding funds to include APT during future academic years. Teachers have acquired skills in leading improvisations and staging that will stay with them for the rest of their teaching careers. They have also come to appreciate the value of acting out scenes from novels. Decision makers discovered the utility of the program as a component of their school reform plans.

An outgrowth of Urban Writes is Teachers' Place, a professional development program designed to help teachers acquire skill as directors and interpreters of drama. APT gained new supporters from the philanthropic world to establish this program designed for high school teachers who want to integrate theatre into their instructional programs. Teaching artists broadened their knowledge of high school and explored another career option as teaching artists.

Student attendance in English classes improved by more than 10 percent during the Urban Writes sessions. Interviews confirmed a direct cause-and-effect relationship between absence and cutting and Urban Writes sessions. Students' attitudes toward themselves and others were clearly influenced by their participation in Urban Writes. When interviewed during an intermission of the year's final production, they told how they had become regular theatregoers, taking advantage of the several discount programs available through the school. They talked about how cool it was to see live action on the stage. Students who participated directly in Urban Writes talked about how they never thought they would perform on the stage in front of their peers. They talked about learning to move on the stage in a more coordinated way and mentioned how scary it was at first. They talked about feeling triumphant after doing their bit and receiving loud applause from the audience. They talked about the camaraderie that developed with classmates looking out for each other. Much of the comparisons between before the program and after could be traced to Urban Writes, although other factors were at work as well. For example, students are older now than they were at the onset of the program. They can go out on their own more; they require (or insist on) less parental supervision. Consequently, more students made the effort to catch performances at off-Broadway theatres more readily.

It took three years to realize the vision APT had when writing the proposal to the NEA. Those considering similar initiatives in inner-city high schools should keep the history of Urban Writes in mind as they plan. Good work takes time to develop.

Lessons Learned

Following is a "to-do" list derived from the lessons learned from the pilot project, Urban Writes. The list is applicable to many other projects that may be more or less ambitious.

1. *Convene participants for a one-day retreat.* This is the key technique for getting all key people on the same page at the start of the project. No amount of short planning sessions accomplishes what can be done in a well-planned day away from the distractions of school.

2. *Develop a letter of agreement between the school and its partner, cosigned by the administrators of each entity.* I am a true believer in the power of the written word, and when things go wrong, it is always helpful to see what the contract said regarding allocated responsibilities. Although it is understood that the contract is not a legal document, it does allow everyone to enumerate expectations and responsibilities. Some organizations like to draw up a contract between students and the organization. These documents are usually drawn up as a strategy to deal with poor classroom management. I have rarely seen the documents achieve what good planning and good pedagogy can accomplish. What is useful, however, is a printed description of the program's outlines, expectations, and anticipated outcomes. This kind of communiqué between program officers and teachers and students can be an attractive jumping-off point from which to begin the residency.

3. *If students are expected to write original scenes and small plays, there must be a playwright and director as part of the theatre's team of resident artists.*

4. *If students are to keep journals or portfolio documentation of personal progress, then the entries need to be periodically reviewed and commented upon.* Students should be encouraged to write to particular prompts that require thoughtful and detailed responses. They would be helped if they had a portfolio rubric to guide their work, but the rubric needs to be well crafted and not just a verbal

statement of degrees. Students need examples of high-scoring entries so they can model their own accordingly.

5. *Convene regular on-site staff meetings.*
6. *Ensure a post performance reflection activity.* Structure the reflective process so that at the end of the process, students can see what worked, what needed more work, and what would be appropriate next steps in their development as students for whom theatre education was important.

Other High School Projects

As director of the School Arts Rescue Initiative (SARI), I had the pleasure of observing some outstanding programs for high school students who were still enduring some of the symptoms of post-traumatic stress syndrome. At Hoboken High School, not far from the riverfront from which they could see the attack on the World Trade Center towers, students discovered some solace in creative work. They developed documentaries about their lives in their own neighborhoods, and in doing so, they were inspired to do historical research, script writing, and editing under the guidance of professional filmmakers from The Kitchen, a cutting-edge performing and visual arts center in Soho, New York City. They also found by participating in dance class with artists from the Alvin Ailey American Dance Theatre a release for their pent-up energies. They learned repertoire that is part of the Ailey legacy, and by learning movements from *Revelations* and other Ailey classics, they discovered an unexpected doorway to African-American history. This school, thanks to the enthusiastic leadership of Paula Ohaus, arts coordinator, and the support of the principal and district superintendent, is well on its way to becoming an island of excellence.

In Valley Stream, Long Island, SARI provided support to help launch a longed-for arts-centered high school, a magnet to students wanting to immerse themselves in the arts as part of their college preparatory program. Valley Stream was particularly hard hit by the collapse of the Twin Towers, losing residents who worked in the building as well as firefighters who lost their lives trying to save others. In a collaborative project between the schools and community, students created and installed a memorial sculpture and orchestrated a memorial service with a student performance choreographed and coached by artists from the Martha Graham Company. The entire experience taught participants how the arts help us bear the unbearable and direct ourselves toward a future despite our grief. Central High School is now the arts high school in Valley Stream and delivers an arts curriculum that includes not only theatre but also art, music, and dance.

Developing arts curricula in high schools is often an effort tied to creating three-year sequences for arts majors that will help students enter arts-centered institutes of higher education. Arts-infused curricula are harder to implement because of the constraints of typical high schools. But as alternative designs for high schools increase in number as small schools, magnets, and specialized arts high schools, new arts-infused curricula are appearing on websites and in research literature. This is all very good news because the high schools are so greatly in need of expressive outlets for students who have a lot to say but are not always articulate.

Integrated Learning 7

R eaders of this book cannot browse through most chapters without bumping into recurring references to the integrated or arts-infused curriculum. When discussing educational reform and the need to update and enhance the curriculum of public schools, there lies the integrated curriculum. If one discusses the role of outside agencies as partners in learning with schools, there sits the integrated curriculum. And when we examine the role of artists as resources in the learning process, we cannot avoid the importance of the integrated curriculum. So much power is ascribed to the integrated curriculum, and so little is known regarding how it impacts on either school or individual improvement.

Definition of an Arts-Integrated Curriculum

I have been working on a universal definition of an integrated curriculum for years. The closest I have come to a "one definition covers all" description is as follows:

An *integrated curriculum* contains intended teaching practices and learning outcomes wherein one academic domain is interlaced with other domains or subject areas for the acquisition of new knowledge or skills or greater understanding of existing knowledge or skills.

When discussing an *arts-integrated curriculum*, the usual definition suggests that the arts are infused or injected into a nonarts subject or domain. But there are many obvious opportunities to infuse historical or mathematical or scientific knowledge into an arts domain. Consequently, it is important to consider an arts-integrated curriculum as multidirectional. Because the arts are present in most aspects of knowledge, especially if design is included in the content of the word *arts*, it should follow that infusing the arts into the study of math or science, technology, or the humanities simply repacks knowledge into its original wrappings.

The usual claim for an arts-integrated curriculum is that a student will learn better a nonarts subject such as reading or math if one or more of the arts are brought into the mix. Therefore, implicit in the definition of an arts-integrated curriculum is a corollary that implies improved learning. Describing the attributes and advantages of an arts-integrated curriculum, however, does not guarantee adequate practice of same. The challenge to both those who develop curriculum guides and standards as well as to those who teach them is to ensure that in the process of arts integration, the meat of each discipline is not replaced by sawdust.

Frequently an arts-integrated curriculum is subdivided into thematic units that require guest teachers, team teaching, or the extensive use of extra-classroom resources that augment the expertise of the single teacher in front of the class. In the best situations, the teacher works with additional resources (beyond the textbook) to deliver a teaching scenario in which students engage in project-based or active learning in which the arts take an important role. Such a scenario needs to be complemented, however, by rigorous instruction in the artistic as well as academic domains. Asking youngsters to create copper plaques based on illustrations in a social studies textbook does not provide art instruction. It merely helps children transfer an image from one plane to another. If, however, in the process of transferring images, new artistic skills such as gridding and resizing are introduced, at least the children are acquiring a skill that is used in making art. Better yet, if the class examines the illustrations for their aesthetic qualities, and figures out how the artist created the original images, and then uses that information to enhance their own illustrations, true integration of art and historical interpretation is approached.

Origins of Today's Push for an Arts-Integrated Curriculum

Advocacy of an arts-integrated curriculum for the education of every child emerged as a strategy to combat escalating cuts of arts programs nationwide during the late 1960s and '70s. The establishment of the arts in education category in federal and state education departments was designed to promote efforts to improve schools. As advocacy for arts-integrated programs gained momentum, the idea developed a life of its own under the title Arts in Education. Coined during the Johnson administration, it is used now as a synonym for a curriculum that contains many arts-related activities usually requiring the services of cultural institutions, resident artists, musicians, playwrights, dancers, or actors and dependent on outside funding, or a reallocation of existing resources such as district funds for curriculum development, professional development, or categorical or competitive grants, awards, and partnerships with corporate and private sponsors.

A variety of national and regional curriculum models have emerged over the past three decades, each claiming the power to serve two goals: (1) improved learning and (2) stronger support for the legitimacy of a full arts curriculum in every school. National foundations have assisted in funding model programs since the 1960s, and such names as Ford, Rockefeller, Annenberg, and Getty have long been associated with the promotion of arts-integrated curricula. Local and regional family foundations have also fostered arts-integrated curriculum development. A leading force for arts integration have been the state and local arts councils or commissions. They have been particularly supportive of programs that employ artists and arts organizations in support of learning through the arts.

For the past three years, the U.S. Department of Education has awarded grants to school districts to assist in the development of model arts-integrated curricula. One of these programs is Tucson's "Opening Minds Through the Arts," or OMA, a consortium consisting of the Tucson Symphony, Tucson Opera, the University of Arizona, and the Tucson Arts Connection. This program's purpose is to expand an integrated curriculum for teachers and artists focused on music through all grades. The project is well described on the Internet [*www.omaproject.org*] and includes a summary of evaluation findings to date.

Other recipients of recent rounds of grants from the U.S. Department of Education, ranging from around $500,000 to $1 million each, were the Rockford, IL, Public Schools, the Mississippi Arts Commission (a state arts agency), and ArtsConnection in New York City for "Investigating the Arts and Literacy Connection."

The Alliance for a Media Literate America (AMLA), in partnership with Just Think, a San Francisco-based media education nonprofit, was granted funds to implement a three-year Media Arts education program suitable for grades six to eight to be piloted in two low-income middle schools in San Francisco and evaluated by outside professionals. Through this project, the AMLA and Just Think are creating an innovative model curriculum demonstrating the effectiveness of integrating Media Arts into the core middle school curriculum to strengthen arts instruction and improve students' academic performance.

The Englewood School District in California and its partners—the Englewood Education Foundation (EEF); the University of Northern Colorado (UNC); Metropolitan State College (MSCD); the Englewood Cultural Arts Center Association (Englewood Arts); the Museum of Outdoor Art (MOA); the David Taylor Dance Theatre (DTDT); Up Close and Musical (UCAM); the Englewood Public Library; and the Englewood Parks and Recreation Center—are combining resources to develop a pilot program. The project provides artists, staff, and students with a teaching and learning model of creative and critical problem-solving through the arts, enabling students to transfer these skills to other core curriculum areas (focusing on literacy). Once established across the curriculum, the model will be accessible to the district's 3800 students PK–12, as well as parents and adult community members.

The California Center for the Arts and the Escondido Foundation (The Center) were given funds to implement project SUAVE: A Model Approach to Teaching English Language Learners Through the Arts. The project intends to further develop, evaluate, and disseminate SUAVE (Socios Unidos Para Artes Via Educación—"United Communities for Arts in Education"), its nationally recognized model arts learning program. The SUAVE project, a collaborative venture of The Center, Cal State San Marcos, and local partner school districts, is an educational and cultural partnership designed to infuse the arts into core curriculum instruction in multicultural and multilingual settings. SUAVE pairs The Center's resident artists, called "arts coaches," with classroom teachers to develop strategies that integrate multiple disciplines—visual arts, music, dance, theater—into instruction of core subjects such as language arts, mathematics, science, and social studies, and also develop knowledge of the arts in and of themselves.

The goal of the SmART School project, housed at the Education Development Center, Inc. (EDC), is to strengthen both the place of the arts as a core academic subject in the regular curriculum and the use of high-quality arts in other academic subjects. SmART Schools is a standards-based, whole-school change model with five key design features:

1. Daily instruction in the arts.
2. Arts integration (teaching for understanding in and through the arts).
3. Professional development that builds a powerful learning community.
4. An inclusive school culture that supports arts-infused education.
5. Active parent/community involvement.

Each of the participating schools is utilizing the America's Choice Comprehensive School Reform Model, in which a literacy coach assists teachers in implementing creative strategies to promote improvements in English language arts and math performance. In each school, an arts specialist coordinates and collaborates with the literacy coach to integrate the arts with core curriculum in English language arts and, in selected schools, in math, social studies, science, and technology. Curriculum revolves around a theme, using the particular art genre specific to each school.

The funded programs have much in common, including the equal emphasis on learning in the arts and learning through the arts; hiring personnel who can lend their expertise as teachers, artists, and curriculum developers and evaluators to help formulate and implement the programs; and an oversight process that monitors quality and intervenes when quality maintenance becomes an issue.

In my own experience, working with New Rochelle and Teaneck, as well as Jefferson County, Kentucky, the major factor—given strong local advocacy—was the marshaling of support from various local, regional, state, and federal grant programs. This support resulted in networking the districts into the inner circle of high-profile arts education grantees. The more these districts acquired support, the more support they were given. No one likes to fund a program that does not promise success. Consequently, the schools cited in these reports tend to be on a lot of donors' lists for support.

Common Pitfalls in an Arts-Integrated Instructional Program

When I was teaching history in junior high school, I would often see arts projects suggested at the end of a textbook chapter as Recommended Activities for Follow-Up. While the suggestions were in many instances intriguing ("Create a diorama" or "Paint a mural" or "Write a play" or "Choreograph a dance"), nowhere was there a discussion of what would be needed in order to help youngsters successfully complete one of these suggested activities. Only when the arts-integrated curriculum movement gained recognition was there the opportunity to examine what was really necessary in order to complete these typical enrichment activities with some kind of artistic and intellectual dimension. I have observed too many "integrated arts projects" where students followed simplistic directions regarding how they should make an object that is in some way related to a geographic or historical topic without any research or substantive instruction in creating the object. On the other hand, when I visited a kindergarten class that had constructed a scaled reproduction of a plains Indian teepee, because of the way the project was managed by the teacher and teaching artist, the kids could tell me with great conviction and accuracy who lived in a structure like the one they created, and how they cooked, slept, and kept their teepee clean!

Rationale for Arts-Integrated Curricula

Arts education advocates cite many substantive reasons to integrate the arts:

- The arts make the textbook study of a topic come alive; children therefore learn more and with enthusiasm.
- Art-making is a form of active learning, combining research with demonstration of knowledge (the project) in a joyful atmosphere.
- Arts education gives students opportunities to manipulate ideas and materials to engage more effectively in intellectual inquiry.
- Students who are regularly and intensely engaged in the arts tend to be the same students who score well on standardized tests, regardless of their family income.
- When the arts are allied with basic skills instruction, the arts are less likely to be removed from the school during budget crunches.
- Learning through the arts helps students acquire skills that may be transferable to the workplace.
- Learning through the arts promotes positive socialization of children from different ethnic and racial groups as well as children from different economic striations.

Several of these claims have become the basis of sizeable research projects over the past ten years. In the most prominent publication, *Champions of Change*, claims regarding the arts and learning were substantiated in separate chapters summarizing research conducted by James Catterwall and Shirley Brice. Each showed a strong relationship between the arts and academic achievement, especially in populations of at-risk youngsters.

When I was involved with the New York City school system as manager of the Arts in General Education (AGE) program, we collaborated with the New York Foundation for the Arts in a funded program that put together teams of artists with different specialties and different racial identities and sent them out to AGE schools for extended periods of time. The object of this Elementary and Secondary Assistance Act (ESAA)–funded project was to explore with schools ways to get kids from different groups to work together creating multidimensional works of art under the leadership and expert guidance of artists who acted as role models of cooperation across lines of difference. The project involved young artists who subsequently earned national reputations for their artistic achievements. Their work was extremely demanding, and yet they persevered, inventing new ways to work as artists as well as new ways to work as educators. Among the members of the ESAA team were Tony award–winning actress Trazana Beverly; Nuyorican Poets Cafe founder Miguel Algarin; theater producer Carl Clay; storyteller Laura Simms; painter and actor Dan Gibbons; and several well-known designers for the theater and dance. The ESAA artists worked in middle and elementary schools with the most daunting assignment: create multidisciplinary arts events or objects and enhance mutual understanding at the same time. The work that emerged from classrooms where teachers and students collaborated with the ESAA artists made statements that were original and energetically produced if not always polished artistic statements. Students, their teachers, and the artists gained a greater appreciation of the creative act and the power of the arts to bridge gaps between human beings of all shades and classes.

In the practice of integrated arts, we must confront not only the central educational question ("What should students know and be able to do at various stages of their intellectual and social development") but also aesthetic questions related to producing, responding to, and analyzing the arts. Teachers and teaching artists must explore how to develop curricula that maintain valid arts processes and content while being true to the goals of the "other" domain. Without doing so, the practice of integrating the arts into the wider curriculum simply adds more reason to seek educational reform!

Here is a case that illustrates the challenge: Fourth-grade students make a canoe during their social studies class under the leadership of an artist/anthropologist who is well versed in Indian life along the Hudson. The canoe is a scaled-down, beautiful replica of one used to float on the Hudson River during the seventeenth century. Students develop control over unfamiliar tools related to creating three-dimensional objects. They work on the aesthetic aspects of the canoe as well as its functionality. They apply what they have learned in math about scale. Students casually discuss the use of canoes as a form of transportation while making the object, but no in-depth research is required. The canoe is mounted in the foyer of the school building as an example of an arts-integrated experience. What works and what's wrong with this example?

Students clearly enjoyed making the canoe. They learned the techniques and the craft requirements in the process. They did not read related literature regarding life lived in seventeenth century Hudson Valley, and while they could make a few accurate comparisons between life then and now in regard to transportation, they did not acquire the background to analyze general and specific transportation issues, an important aspect of the required social studies standards. If the teacher had elicited from her students concepts about transportation from their experience making the canoe, she could have demonstrated some of the advantages of integration. There was more work to be done by the teacher regarding extending student knowledge about transportation. In this instance, the teacher needed to provide a solid reading list, offer opportunities for small and large discussion groups to formulate ideas regarding transportation, and probe for student knowledge and understanding through tests, quizzes, or other assessment efforts.

The canoe served as a motivation and an opportunity to admire the craftsmanship and knowledge of the river by the Native Americans who lived along the Hudson River. It was also fun, and that is an ingredient not always present in today's classrooms. The challenge for teacher and artist in this project was to build in adequate time for both the arts-making process and the inquiry into the social studies topic.

The arts-integrated unit approach should promote a process of rigorous inquiry, research, and report, and claims of learning need to be consistently verified throughout the process. Many arts-integrated efforts depend on teaming teachers with teaching artists working together within their specialties to help students express ideas and understandings with accuracy, proficiency, and aesthetic effectiveness. Successful efforts emerge from well-thought-out, *written* teaching units that are specific and ensure a high degree of personal and group accountability for the information and skills contained within them. The best units of instruction are those that are prepared by teachers and artists together and are then reviewed for accuracy and rigor by curriculum experts.

Examples abound of art, music, dance, and theater projects that enhance students' understanding and handling of the arts as well as the linked academic area. Some are models of synergy, where the art-making complements and even extends students' understanding of academic material. In some instances, however, the product will have been a fun thing to do or make, but it does no service to either the art or academic disciplines. The trick is to give parity to both the arts and academic content. If parity is not reached, there is a dual danger: Students will spend hours building the canoe during class time instead of covering what they are accountable for. Worse yet, students may be deprived of learning other aspects of the required curriculum because of lack of time. The problem of parity becomes more serious in the upper grades, where high-stakes testing haunts teachers and administrators who dare to consider widening the curriculum or straying from test preparation.

The most numerous examples of arts-integrated curriculum require that the arts be infused into another discipline (e.g., the arts into math, the arts into science, social studies, or English language arts). Rarely is math infused into music or science into art, although these are perfectly legitimate ways to integrate curricula. Art classes can call for the application of knowledge about one domain into an artistic framework. Thus, when students are concentrating on a chain of events that denote an historical watershed in their social studies class, they can be asked to compose a mural depicting key events along a timeline, or a photo essay that conveys the meaning of "community." A music class might be asked to create a discography of musical recordings that stem from the Civil War. A dance class may be encouraged to choreograph a dance that represents the interaction between elements or molecules, based on knowledge acquired in class.

Theatre lends itself particularly well to an integrated curriculum. The content of plays, the writing of plays, production, and criticism all fall within both the domain-centered curriculum as well as the cross-curricular themes such as critical thinking, creative problem solving, conflict resolution, and aesthetic analysis. As John and Evelyn Dewey wrote so many years ago:

> The possibilities for plays, festivals, and pageants . . . are end-
> less; for it is always possible to find subject matter which will
> give the children just as much training in reading, spelling,

history, literature, or even some phases of geography, as would dry Gradgrind facts of a routine textbook type. (97)

It is more likely that the wider curriculum can be pulled into the arts studios than the other way around in secondary schools. It seems to be easier for arts people to pull in ideas from other parts of the curriculum (history, math, science, cultural studies, etc.) than for their test-plagued colleagues to pull the arts into their curriculum. A choral teacher may explore more easily the events of World War I as part of preparing her chorus to sing segments of Benjamin Britten's *War Requiem* than a history teacher can stop his narrative lectures to play and discuss a recording of the same music. (This is not always true, however. Many gifted history teachers would find it not only easy but essential to use examples of music, dance, and theater performances to provide further insight into past events and trends.)

Arts-integrated units usually are organized around a theme that functions as a kind of lens through which the students can investigate various kinds of subject matter. For example, rather than studying math or social studies in isolation, a junior high school class might study a unit called The Sea, researching social studies questions to understand the historical development of seashore communities, economic questions to discover why coastal and inland populations have different livelihoods, and math inquiry to calculate the changes past, current, and future regarding erosion of the seashore. The class might be divided into inquiry groups—each group focusing on an important question to be answered by research and deliberation. Whole-class assignments might include reading Hemingway's *The Old Man and the Sea* and Richard Dana's *After Twenty Years* as well as Melville's *Moby Dick*. Younger classes might watch a DVD of *Finding Nemo*. Class discussions might center on why the sea has such a strong hold on the human imagination. In science class, students should read Rachel Carson's classic *The Sea Around Us*, with an update by marine ecologist, Jeffrey Levinton. They should be expected to bring their various investigations together in a series of class formal and informal reports where by the end of the unit, students have collected enough information to become the basis of true understandings based on newly acquired knowledge. As in the previously mentioned forest unit, students should be encouraged to think of how their new knowledge should be used to construct the future.

In some reform efforts, the curriculum is addressed simply through the selection of textbooks. For example, in the massive New York City school reform effort, "Children First," the Chancellor mandated that all schools follow a prescribed phonics program, *Month by*

Month Phonics (Carson-Dellosa Publishing), and a balanced literacy program to define the day-to-day lessons in reading and the English language. The Chancellor also selected specific math texts: *Everyday Mathematics* (Wright Group/McGraw-Hill) and *Impact Mathematics* (Glencoe/Macmillan McGraw-Hill) for elementary and middle schoolers, accordingly. These texts are, for all intents and purposes, the curriculum. Because of the extended time in elementary schools set aside for reading and math, teachers may opt for activities to augment the curriculum in these subjects with projects that require an infusion of arts production or response or both. Insecure principals are loath to permit this activity, however, because of their fear that by taking students away from the workbooks they will endanger their scores on reading tests. It's as if the workbook is a kind of breathing machine designed for acute care; if the patient is taken off the machine, he might die! We know that patients need to be weaned off the machine if they are ever going to be able to breathe on their own. Even high-performing schools have principals who are afraid to endanger their high scores for fear of losing their preferred place on the school ranking list. With the annual publication of reading scores, a diligent researcher might check to see what kinds of arts programs are in place at low-performing schools. My hunch is that many of the low-performing schools have few if any good arts programs.

Where enlightened teaching occurs, a visitor might see students valuing geometry by becoming involved in an architectural design project that requires them to measure, calculate, estimate, and work with previously learned formulae in order to complete original architectural models. Students might construct models under the guidance of a professional architect or their math teacher or both. Some informal studies in the form of project evaluations have shown that some students tend to score better in standardized testing as a result of adding active learning projects to time on the workbook and text.

Many cities are investing time and money on top-down models of curriculum development, but other reform efforts emphasize site-based management where principals of individual schools determine texts, schedules, and assessment routines as long as they complement the local, state, and national standards. Unfortunately, as with most American reform efforts, the cities tended to institute site-based management systemwide, and inevitably found that it worked well in some sites and miserably in others. Lessons learned regarding site-based management apparently did not include the finding that one size does not fit all.

Lately, the Bush administration has gotten into the text recommending business, denying schools their federal aid unless they use texts that have been approved by the U.S. Department of Education. This policy has undermined many efforts at differentiating schools from each other based on their different strengths and weaknesses. For example, in New York City, the current policy of one curriculum for all is mandated with just two exceptions (to date): (1) Those two hundred or so schools that have very high scores on the reading and math tests may make their own curriculum decisions, and (2) those scoring at the very lowest must use the federally approved program in order to gain the "carrot" of some $34 million from the government.

At various times and places, teachers are invited to "invent curriculum," which involves finding or creating textual material that supports state and local standards and the school/district curricular goals and objectives. Teacher-made curricula usually evolve from a combination of animated brainstorming sessions and painful writing sessions. Rare is the teacher who can write cohesive, coherent teaching aids without additional editorial help from a professional writer/editor. The best efforts for teacher-made curriculum appear to me to be those that provide certain essential ingredients directly related to expertise and sufficient time to complete the tasks involved well. Curriculum developers require:

- Experts in the content and process of learning at the table during all phases of the effort.
- Sufficient time for talking through the purpose of the curriculum guide among those who would "write it."
- Sufficient time for research so that lessons are drawn not just from the imagination but also from solid information with pedagogical procedures suited to the purpose.
- Sufficient time for drafting, responding, revising, piloting, and revising again to meet the goal of the documents.
- Teachers need to feel that their work will be used by their colleagues as well as themselves and should advance everyone's sense of urgency about completing the job.

In my time, I have been involved with many curriculum development efforts. The most successful were always characterized by these conditions. The less-successful efforts where I was invited to be a facilitator of a curriculum writing project were limited by the lack of one or more of these conditions. Primarily, the projects were not given enough time to come to full bloom; they were hastily assembled to meet some external deadline usually connected to a grant. They were rarely given the kind of review that is necessary to get it right, and worse yet, no one really wanted to write, much less use, the curriculum enhancements. These assignments, which I eventually rejected as hopelessly doomed, continue to pop up wherever the grant-making game is involved.

Separate Domains of Instruction and Synchronized Learning

Arts-integrated education should not be confused with sequential instruction in music, art, dance, drama, and media. The arts subjects that we are used to seeing listed in school catalogs usually are taught separately from those efforts where arts integration is the goal. That said, it is not unusual for art teachers, especially in the elementary grades, to consult with teachers and introduce projects that somehow relate to what is happening in the regular classroom. Although arts teachers once feared that the integrationists would supplant traditional instruction in the arts, this fear seems to be mostly unsubstantiated.

One of the unfortunate consequences of employing independent artists in elementary schools has been the "covering" of dance and drama with short-term dance or drama residencies rather than with courses of study that run the whole school year. Principals in more than a few schools check off their arts requirements by citing a ten-week program in dance or drama (translation: a class of four receives forty minutes of instruction ten times) as opposed to a course of study served twice a week for forty to eighty minutes all during the school year.

In secondary schools, students are often asked to choose between an arts sequence of study and another "more academic" sequence such as a three-year foreign language study or an advanced sequence in mathematics or science. The standard high school program does not have enough time set aside for art and advanced academics. The arts, therefore, are closed out as options for the most academically ambitious students and relegated to options for those who seemingly do not wish to study the difficult subjects or to try to get into the more competitive colleges and universities. Academic classes where the arts are infused seem to be the only opportunities these academically driven students have to stretch their aesthetic sensibilities. Meanwhile, those with less academic drive are isolated from their more academically stimulating peers who are tracked for greater success in the world of higher education and business. Ambitious parents and guidance counselors steer college-bound students from arts electives, and the all-school arts events in high school are generally given extracurricular status without the advantage of strong foundation courses for the actors, designers, and directors of the student plays and musicals.

One possible solution to the tension between arts-integrated practices and maintaining the integrity of arts disciplines as their own bodies of knowledge is in what I call *synchronized learning*. Here the responsibility for integration lies with students prompted by teachers who know what is being taught in allied classes as well as in their own. Students who study sculpture as an art elective may start with a study of ancient Greek, Roman, African, and Asian sculpture and proceed through postmodernism, making their own statements according to these conventions. Meanwhile, their history teachers are following a similar chronology and geographic swing. It is then up to the teachers to prompt questions that stimulate students to wed their learnings in art and history and to provide independent projects (papers, portfolios, etc.) that demonstrate understandings related to specific times and cultures.

Reform Efforts and the Arts

When investigating the arts within a context of school reform, one encounters the persistent problem of time. The school day is not long enough; after-school programs are generally badly attended and cannot make up for a mandated seven-hour day. The class sessions are too short to accomplish deep inquiry, continuous feedback from peers and teachers, and opportunities for guided practice and revision of papers and other projects. The arts once again illuminate the needs of schools not only for the arts but also for other features of a successful school. Those schools that have overcome these barriers are the ones that have modified the teaching and learning day and year. The Coalition of Schools, for example, advocates replacing forty-minute class periods with seminar-type classes of an hour or more much like the Core class that I taught thirty-five years ago! With the introduction of the extended day, where credit is granted for classes that go beyond the usual six-hour day, some headway has been made, but extended periods and extended teaching days need to be augmented by extended numbers of days in the academic year. New York has attempted to do this by increasing the number of days and minutes in a day in the contract with the United Federation of Teachers. Time will tell whether these modifications help reduce the conflict for time between the arts and academics.

In the meantime, schools continue to experiment, despite constraints put upon them by the No Child Left Behind Act. By the time this book hits the marketplace, No Child Left Behind may be a relic of the history books or at least sufficiently modified to encourage the creation and maintenance of successful schools. The impulse to rebel, to transform mediocre environments into incubators for talent and achievement will continue, and the integrated curriculum, which has been a valuable tool in all of these reform efforts, will continue to play an important part in efforts to create islands of excellence, models for future reform movements.

Successful Integration Efforts

In evaluating various projects where arts integration is a key element, my associates and I have found a recurring pattern that includes the following:

- We observe situations where the arts reinforce learning in the wider curriculum only when there is a rigorous planning and implementation process that requires teachers to periodically assess anticipated learnings.
- Unless teachers consistently align their teaching with the goals and objectives of the integrated curriculum, we do not see evidence of strong academic or artistic achievement on a classwide basis. What we see are portfolios that are skimpy in content and superficial in analysis, suggesting that there is a deficit in structured, sequential teaching with little to no process for feedback to students about their works in process.
- We see too many examples of integrated learning projects where students are left out of the collaboration. The students simply fulfill a preconceived vision of an arts-integrated project; it is apparent that without their involvement, they have little to no investment in the quality of their own work.
- When teachers design arts-integrated projects, they must rely either on their own multidisciplinary expertise or collaborate with adjunct partners in order to provide a quality experience for their students. With that expertise in place, it is possible to expect students to:
    - *Create* visual, literary, or performance statements (dioramas, murals, portraits, sculptures; prose, poetry, nonfiction, plays; plays, scenes, dances, musicals, etc.) that demonstrate their

understanding of an idea or circumstance that they have learned about.

- *Respond to and interpret* works of art that echo ideas, concepts, and events located within the formal curriculum by finding metaphors and analogies to what they have learned.

An arts-integrated curriculum can be helpful in promoting critical thinking, problem solving, and design thinking. It can launch much more interesting and challenging expository writing as well as exercises in rhetoric. But its potential is reliant on good planning and expert implementation. Otherwise the complications of an arts-integrated curriculum simply result in an extension of the mediocre.

It is important to recognize that efforts to create an arts-integrated curriculum require recognition that complexity alone does not guarantee success. We may be able to do something well that is very simple. We may do something badly because it is too complex. I try to separate issues of excellence from issues of complexity by rating a set of activities along two separate but related continua, one for quality and the other for complexity. It is similar to what the judges in the Olympics do when rating gymnasts or ice skaters. They rate first on technical competence and difficulty of the program, and then they rate on artistic achievement. When we discuss instruction and student performance on an arts-integrated curriculum, we also need to ensure that we are seeing both good art and good education and not confuse issues of complexity with issues of excellence.

So what do we mean by "good art"? And what do we mean by good education? It would be nice if we were to accept the simplistic definition that we know it when we see it, but some of us are satisfied with more than others. Part of the work of educators must be to reach a consensus regarding what is good art as practiced by elementary and middle school students and what is good art as practiced by high schoolers. One thing we know from recent research is that teacher definitions of good art often differ from artists' definitions (Dorn et al.). We also know that that there is a variance regarding what constitutes an effective teacher. Without getting into that argument, I would say that it is at least as important that collaborators on an arts-integrated curriculum need to come to agreement regarding quality and then set forth to elicit quality from their students.

We do know that good education is going on in a classroom when we see kids thinking, wrestling with knowledge, putting knowledge to work, and acquiring knowledge or when we see kids focused on the material as well as the teacher. We know it is not too good when every kid wants to get out of class; the buzz of noise is from escaping rather than engaging with what is happening in the room, when half the class is asleep and the other is talking in and around the teacher who, in turn, is talking to no one in particular or is yelling at everyone. Many of us are more comfortable citing examples of bad education than in describing good education. Once there is consensus regarding art and education, it is then appropriate to proceed to our next chapter, an exploration of program evaluation and assessment of achievement.

8 Evaluation and Assessment

*T*his chapter discusses some of the thorny issues related to the push for program evaluation and assessment of student achievement. It is not a how-to chapter, but it will refer readers to many sources of information regarding evaluation and assessment designs, instruments to measure progress, and ways of interpreting the quality of programming and the immediate effect of programs on students.

The topics of evaluation and assessment have been hot-button items since I first encountered the phenomenon of arts in education. Because of the tendency to advocate for the arts as a remedy for academic or social failure in the schools, there has been a consistent cry for proof that the arts make a difference. Hence the need for rigorous tracking of the influence of the arts on various segments of education—attendance, academic performance, attitude toward self and others, the learning environment, leadership—everything it seems but home cooking! In other words, the cry for evaluation and assessment has also been the cry for validation of the arts in the mandated curriculum for all students, all levels, in all schools.

I have always tried to make a distinction between evaluation (i.e., the process of judging the quality of program elements) and assessment (i.e., the process of measuring the effects of program elements on behavior—students' or teachers' or other targeted populations identified by the programmers). In making judgments about any educational program, we generally look at the program's written description, usually found in a proposal that has been funded. We check to see whether the program described is the program offered, and if there are changes, we probe for the rationale for such changes. We look at the proposed outcomes and try to find evidence that the outcomes are being worked on (formative evaluation) or, if the program has been completed, whether the anticipated outcomes have been reached. We may look at student portfolios, teacher and/or student logs, or other documentation for evidence of program impact.

In evaluating most arts in education programs, we look at staffing, roles and functions, instructional materials used, and actual transactions between program participants. We interview key people associated with the program (e.g., teachers, teaching artists, students, and site-based and general administrators) who represent all entities participating in the program. We look for evidence that, if the program is about an arts-integrated effort, there is evidence of good art work as well as good academic work. If problems are revealed—and there are almost always problems—we address them with project coordinators or their superiors in a way that helps them both recognize and then attempt to solve the perceived problems. Our work is purposely consultative as opposed to being merely judgmental. We like to share what we find as we go along.

Assessments call for specific evidence that shows the ongoing or cumulative effects of the program on the targeted population within the context of the proposed program. If the premise is that an arts-integrated curriculum will elevate student scores on reading tests, then we look at the scores *and* compare them with either the scores of similar populations who did not get the program, *or* compare them with scores before the program began, *or* compare the scores with the average score for a grade in the treatment school or a national norm. If we examine portfolios and the scores they have received by their teachers, we look for some pattern or sign of impact. We also look to see whether the rubrics used to rate portfolios are sufficient to assess student progress accurately. And we ask teachers and teaching artists to comment on student outcomes. Assessment specialists try to use procedures that are specific to an artistic discipline and use the state, local, or national standards as a guide for formulating assessment instruments. Unfortunately, most standards are codified regarding what students are expected to know and do at various grade levels, but there is scant literature regarding quality indicators that help assessors to determine outstanding, as opposed to typical, work in art, music, dance, or drama. Nonetheless, if the assessment specialist is well versed in artistic accomplishment by age or grade, he or she should be able to make some cogent comments regarding the degree to which all, some, or a few students demonstrate particular skills or talents. The 1997 National Assessment of Education Progress in the Arts is somewhat helpful as a model of assessment procedures and findings and could be adapted by assessment specialists.

I first became familiar with the idea of evaluation in graduate school when we were trained how to write lesson plans and thematic resource units. We were required to include procedures that would help us determine whether our students understood what we thought we were teaching, and whether they could apply new knowledge to appropriate situations. We learned how to construct simple tests, and we became familiar with other (soon to be called *alternative*) procedures to measure our impact on learning. With the introduction of proposal writing for federal funding and state regranting, it was incumbent on all of us who wanted to compete for money to experiment with new teaching techniques to learn the lingo of evaluation and include it in our hefty requests to program officers in the state capitol or in Washington.

I got deeply involved in evaluation as a key aspect of arts education when I was manager of the New York City Arts in General Education (AGE) project. Under the facilitative leadership of colleagues at the JDR 3rd Fund, I met some of the major figures in evaluation and research in the country, those who were invited to look at arts education and arts in education and devise defensible data-gathering techniques that would "prove" the importance of the arts in the total educational process. I met Robert Stake, a poetic scientist who showed me that one could record transactions over time in order to determine whether key behaviors were changing as a result of the infusion of the arts into the educational potion. I was introduced to John Goodlad of UCLA and Jerrold Ross, then of NYU, and others, each of whom had a particular view of schools, schooling, and the force of evaluation. My job was to identify schools for a demonstration project (AGE) and at the same time figure out, for proposals, what we would do to show the impact of various project elements on targeted schools. With my colleagues from the JDR 3rd Fund and the New York Foundation for the Arts, I tried to accommodate the requirements of state and federal funders and at the same time put together elements that would strengthen instruction both in the arts and through the arts. Of course, as with so many other programs such as ours, we were encouraged to pick schools that had already demonstrated their support of the arts. This made it very difficult to "prove" that the arts made a difference over a period of time in the change of school climate, student or teacher performance, or leadership. Nonetheless, as with many grant programs, the idea was to pick schools that were winners, not schools that were in deep trouble.

So intrigued was I by the challenge of evaluation that, when invited to apply to NYU's School of Education to complete a doctoral program, I accepted, and left the AGE project at the conclusion of its third year. My course work and research helped bolster my knowledge and skill in this area, and ultimately, my dissertation grew from an evaluation of New York City's next version of arts in education, Arts Partners, a jointly administered program sponsored by the New York City Board of Education, the city's Department of Youth Services, and the Department of Cultural Affairs. The Mayor's office loosened funds that were allocated to some hundreds of schools, which received various arts services through scores of arts organizations in the city. I was asked to evaluate the effectiveness of the partnerships, the power of the concept of interagency collaboration, the impact of certain kinds of residencies on reading test results, and the impact of professional development on teaching artists. My dissertation looked at the often-cited claim that the arts support the development of critical thinking and problem solving and creative thinking (frequently bunched together as higher-level thinking skills). We set up a situation where selected artists were given some modest training in cognitive development and then asked to develop and deliver units of instruction that would elicit higher-level thinking from participating students. We developed observation instruments to assess student transactions during the various residencies and analyzed various kinds of standardized measures as well as questionnaires I developed to see what resulted from the artists' direct instruction.

The most important findings in this study related to the ways in which different artists triggered higher-level thinking in their students and the different levels of thinking that resulted from artists' encouragement of student art making. We found that some artists were much better than others in triggering higher-level thinking. And, not surprising, we found that different artists elicited different levels of creative thinking, problem solving, and critical thinking. The study not only earned me my doctorate, but it also garnered some recognition with its inclusion in the NEA-sponsored compendium of research, *Schools, Communities and the Arts,* juried and edited by the Morrison Institute of Arizona State University. Both before and after Arts Partners, I was asked to evaluate scores of other partnerships between arts organizations and schools in various parts of the country and abroad. And I soon found out that, apart from generating data that tried to align "treatment" with "results," my role was really one of a talking mirror, telling project people what I was seeing, what problems I thought they needed to attend to, what situations were brewing that could create a crisis, and how excellent work could be highlighted as models of effective practice. It was exhausting work, but immensely rewarding as I observed programs growing from innocuous escapes from the daily grind to essential elements of successful schools. In comparison with the national movement toward developing legitimacy in the education community, my work was about how to make the opportunity of arts in the schools most effective. To the degree that my published work advanced the agenda of arts education, I was grateful. But I was never interested in participating in one of the mega-studies that would try to prove the importance of arts education, primarily because I felt that others could do that better than I, and I have yet to be convinced that proving the value of the arts will convince those who will not make even weak efforts to support arts education in their schools.

I have always been most comfortable looking at students engaged at work in a classroom or studio setting, noting the degree to which all, some, or a few are engaged in creative work. I like to look at the works-in-progress and apply my mental template: are they merely following directions or are they investing part of themselves in their work? Are they asking questions of themselves and their instructors to help clarify what they are trying to accomplish? Is their work reflective of a genuine voice or merely a docile response to the teacher's directed instruction. Many of the questions arise from years of experience in observing good, bad, and indifferent situations. Many conclusions are drawn by juxtaposing observations of student behavior with what we researchers know are signs of engagement in higher-level thinking. I would listen to conversations and watch students draw or paint, improvise, or critique each other to see whether they are weighing choices, making comparisons, trying out ideas and evaluating them, putting themselves in the place of their characters, or trying to synthesize a series of experiences into one statement. I would count instances of certain behaviors (teachers' or students' or both), rate numerically the quality of what we observed, and in that way begin to put some quantitative data as well as qualitative data on the table for analysis. I generally engage an artist to work with me so that together we provide an aesthetic as well as pedagogic approach to what we observe and conclude.

Evaluation and Assessment Findings and Accountability

Arts advocates have happily gotten on the bandwagon for accountability, riding the two horses of high-stakes testing and, more reluctantly, Draconian responses to test results. Their thinking—wrongheaded as it may be—is that if the arts played by the same rules as other academic subjects, more schools and more school districts will treat the instruction of art, music, dance, and drama with respect. This has yet to be proved.

Meanwhile, arts organizations and schools in partnerships with them are subject to greater scrutiny than ever before. This is not necessarily bad news, because it is one of the embarrassing secrets of partnerships that without a mandate for rigorous evaluation, most schools would rarely examine the quality or effects of collaboration between artists and teachers in an orderly and structured method.

Nuts and Bolts of Assessment

In the current educational parlance, three kinds of assessment procedures dominate the field: (1) testing dependent on verbal and/or mathematical responses to various kinds of items; (2) performance assessment, wherein students are asked to demonstrate their knowledge through presentation of portfolios or projects for critical analysis; and (3) authentic assessment where student work is examined in situ, analyzed for various criteria, and given some kind of mark representing its value.

Assessment is used at times to diagnose learning needs, establish eligibility for certain programs or classes, and determine and track achievement benchmarks over time. At its most controversial, assessment is linked with measures of individual or school accountability, leading to the rating of teachers and the ranking of schools. There are bookshelves loaded with scholarly works on assessment as well as practical approaches to the selection of the right instruments for use with particular assessment goals. Traditionally, two kinds of assessment have dominated educational practice: classroom tests and standardized tests. Before the 1980s, elementary students endured the classic teacher-made Friday test in which all subjects taught during the preceding week were the substance of short and long answer items. Then, at some point during the second half of the school year, students would be given state- or city-sponsored standardized tests in reading, math, sometimes social studies, rarely science, and possibly a general skills test. The standardized tests would help a teacher determine the needs of her or his students and would in the aggregate contribute to a local ranking process of public schools within a district and in the state. A new wrinkle in assessment was introduced in the 1980s with the publication of Howard Gardner's critique of traditional standardized testing as an unfair and inappropriate measure of intelligence and the experimental Arts Propel project, funded by the Rockefeller Foundation and managed by Project Zero. Within a few years, the portfolio and other kinds of performance assessment were proposed by some schools, districts, and states as an addition or replacement for certain standardized measures.

In recent years, as results of performance assessment have been evaluated, it has become clear that the road to defensible alternative assessment of ability is a rocky one. Although the idea of rating student work on rubrics fashioned by schools, districts, or even states is compelling, making judgments using the rubrics is problematic. Establishing the meaning of rubric cells is much more difficult than attaching a value to a right answer. What looks like an excellent response to one judge in one area can look like an appalling example of high mediocrity to another. When used as a substitute rather than as an adjunct to standardized tests, some of us are concerned that the fine art of memorizing information for later application may be eroded.

Many advocates of performance assessment point to the arts as the source of wisdom, which is flattering to arts advocates but misleading nonetheless. Judging a student's skills and thinking ability by examining a painting or series of sketches leading up to a painting may be analogous to creating a composition in English class, but it is not analogous to the more factually laden aspects of science and mathematics, history and geography, where students need to be tested on what they know as well as what they can do with that knowledge. I want students to know where Iraq is on the globe, and I want them to know how the geography of that country has influenced the development of its social and political structures. I want them to be able to interpret information as presented in the media. I will need to test for that as well as respond to a project demonstration that they have organized as part of their social studies requirement.

Assessment Dilemmas

OLD WINE IN NEW BOTTLES

The portfolio has always been a popular technique for assessing student art or literary work when compiled in a structured and purposeful sequence. As a physical trail of thinking, it can be enormously interesting and helpful in figuring out how a student is progressing. If, on the other hand, it is just a collection of unrelated, so-called "best work" with no indication of what has preceded it, the teacher will find it difficult to track a learning arc.

Some of us who were impressed with the result of the 1980s Arts Propel experiment cautioned our colleagues not to forget how much expertise, extra time, and training were invested in this alternative method of assessing student growth. Teachers were trained not only in how to rate portfolio documents, but also in how to organize their teaching and collection methods to result in appropriate documentation. Many thousands of dollars were spent to buy time for after-school conferences with students as well as for periodic training and information sharing. To separate the portfolio from its developmental processes is to do once more what is so common in American public education: to take the top off the ice cream cone and to disregard the base.

The old idea of collecting student work to show at Open School Night remains pretty much what current practice in portfolio assessment entails. In those instances where real time and effort are put into the collection and analysis of evidence of personal, intensive instruction, the portfolio is a valuable assessment process. It helps to document the learning arc accurately.

PROCESSES AND PRODUCTS

Arts educators in school districts around the country have developed standards for measuring the performance of their students in dance, art, music, and drama. In most cases, the standards and accompanying assessment rubrics have been designed to describe quality and competency. In the best situations, the faculty is trained to use these tools, because the future of their students is in their hands. Enlightened texts have been written for practitioners (by Donna Beattie, Arthur Kosta, Bob Marzano, James Popham, Jay Tighe, etc.) to help district coordinators invent site-specific observation and test instruments. But all the tools require seasoned judgment.

THEORY INFORMED BY PRACTICE

I was recently privy to a high school faculty discussion on grading. They raised all the typical questions: How many characteristics should be measured? What happens when the student works really well in class, tries, but just doesn't have the talent to get a score sufficiently high to pass? What is pass? Why is a student taking an arts sequence anyway? At what point is it fair to say that a student's credits should be denied?

These conundrums are especially troubling for teachers in arts magnet high schools, where the stakes for graduation are increasingly high. Here arts credits are most assuredly going to be used as part of the preparation for an institution of higher education, whether an arts college or liberal arts institution. Suppose the magnet high school accepts students because they love the arts but are not necessarily good practitioners. They are great audience but not necessarily great performers. They love going to museums and even trying their hand at painting and drawing and sculpture, but beyond a certain point, they just don't have it. The paradox of assessment and developing appropriate curriculum standards makes the grading situation even more difficult for conscientious teachers in high schools, where grades have life-affecting consequences.

Leaders in the fields of both the arts and education may have created more problems than they intended when they joined the standards movement. With good intentions, they demanded that the arts be treated just the way other important subjects were to be treated. The visual arts, dance (choreography, technique, improvisation), drama (improvisation, voice, diction, characterization, style, playwriting), and music (voice, instrumental, ensemble performances, virtuosity, technique) demand a panoply of skills and a well-developed intellect that goes beyond performing in a class play or painting the scenery for it. Sequential arts programming demands time on task, in some kind of logical sequence; yet the arts curricula are frequently not sequential but colinear, multilayered rather than spiraled. How many art classes start and end with unrelated projects, each representing a different bank of skills (a still life watercolor, followed by a record cover, followed by a portrait in charcoal, followed by whatever...). As we know in theatre education, one learns to do something and practice it at one developmental level and the following year, as one's voice and body change, the exercises become more complicated even though the person is basically the same in tenth grade as he or she was in the sixth grade.

THE FALSE DICHOTOMY OF PROCESS VERSUS PRODUCT

And then we have the false dichotomy of process versus product, as usually voiced by elementary school teachers and teaching artists who are forced to assess the merits of students' creative work. The arguments range from: "Why do our kids have to undergo the rough treatment of assessment in the arts? Can't they just do the arts for fun and as an escape from the pressures of the rest of the test-driven day? Why must we look so carefully at the products—the paintings, the poetry, the plays as written and performed, the elementary ensemble concerts—when the artistic process is important." For me, the product has to be an index to the process. If the concert is painful to listen to, then the instructional process was certainly misguided. If the dancers are whirling around with no pattern or center, something was clearly wrong with the choreographic process. If the poem sounds more like a fifty-year-old than a seventeen-year-old, we must ask where the genuine voice is and whether the process was imitative or creative and value it accordingly.

SAMPLE INSTRUMENTS

The evaluation instruments included here are generic versions of those that we have adapted for various performing arts companies or visual arts organizations that have partnered with schools over long periods of time. In developing these forms, I usually work with artists connected to the projects to make site-specific modifications. Nasha Thomas Schmitt of the Alvin Ailey Dance Theater Foundation and Ann Biddle, consultant to the Ballet Hispanico Company, were particularly helpful in the construction of evaluation instruments for dance. The instruments are also reflections of what various researchers (including myself) have cited as critical elements in cognitive or affective growth (see Figures 8–1 through 8–5).

Figure 8–1   Typical Evaluation/Assessment Design

Hypotheses or Claims	Procedure to Develop Evidence
1. The arts contribute to emotional stability (e.g., improved self-esteem, better classroom behavior, etc.).	Standardized self-esteem questionnaires (such as Bracken's *Multidimensional Self Concept Scale*) Project developed questionnaires Structured observations and/or interviews over time by experts including sociograms (such as *BRACE*, developed by Bank Street College of Education)
2. The arts contribute to better understanding of other domains of learning.	Pre- and post-tests on academic subject matter (standardized and site-specific) Analysis of report card marks Analysis of anecdotal records (teacher's, student's) Portfolio analysis Classroom observations by experts using checklist correlated to academic transactions
3. The arts lead to better understanding of self and others.	Interviews with participants over time Observations over time Project protocols that align with self-understanding checklists
4. The arts contribute to cognitive development (e.g., critical thinking, problem solving, decision making, analysis, synthesis, etc.)	Standardized tests on thinking skills (e.g., *Ross Test of Higher Cognitive Processes* or McGraw-Hill's *Terra Nova* battery of tests or tests used by local school district as part of its accountability design) Observation of transactions in class (e.g., Classroom Observation Checklist by S. Lee Winocur in Costa's *Developing Performance Assessments*) Comparison of classes with and without arts treatment

Figure 8–2 Dance Assessment Checklist

Name: _____ **Group:** _____

Artist's name: _____

Teaching partner's name: _____

Discipline (circle one): **Ballet** **Jazz** **Modern** **Tap**

Techniques of Performance:

Directions: To be filled out by *artist and teaching partner* together. For each student selected for assessment, fill out column one at the beginning of the instructional program. At the end of the program, fill out column two. Use this scale:
0 = not applicable; 1 = not evident (but should have been); 2 = poor; 3 = fair; 4 = good; 5 = excellent. Please indicate the difference (+ or –) between the camper at the beginning and end of camp in the "change" column.

#	Item	At Beginning of Program	At End of Program	Change +/-
	Dance technique			
	When asked to do so, student ...			
1.	Enters and exits dance studio in an appropriate manner.	0 1 2 3 4 5	0 1 2 3 4 5	
2.	Maintains personal space.	0 1 2 3 4 5	0 1 2 3 4 5	
3.	Travels in general space without bumping.	0 1 2 3 4 5	0 1 2 3 4 5	
4.	Assumes correct positions.	0 1 2 3 4 5	0 1 2 3 4 5	
5.	Repeats dance phrases accurately.	0 1 2 3 4 5	0 1 2 3 4 5	
6.	Displays appropriate dance energy.	0 1 2 3 4 5	0 1 2 3 4 5	
7.	Demonstrates clear direction changes.	0 1 2 3 4 5	0 1 2 3 4 5	
8.	Demonstrates a variety of efforts (movement qualities).	0 1 2 3 4 5	0 1 2 3 4 5	
9.	Demonstrates different relationships (duets, trios, small groups).	0 1 2 3 4 5	0 1 2 3 4 5	
10.	Responds well to feedback from teachers & peers.	0 1 2 3 4 5	0 1 2 3 4 5	
11.	Reaches a performance standard that interprets the choreographer's vision.	0 1 2 3 4 5	0 1 2 3 4 5	

continues

Figure 8–2   continued

#	Item	At Beginning of Program	At End of Program	Change +/–
	Character			
	Without being prompted, student ...			
12.	Acknowledges the progress of self and others.	0 1 2 3 4 5	0 1 2 3 4 5	
13.	Gets along well with others in class.	0 1 2 3 4 5	0 1 2 3 4 5	
14.	Shows respect for artist.	0 1 2 3 4 5	0 1 2 3 4 5	
15.	Shows respect for group leader.	0 1 2 3 4 5	0 1 2 3 4 5	
16.	Maintains positive behavior during rehearsals.	0 1 2 3 4 5	0 1 2 3 4 5	
	Total points			
	Comments:			

Figure 8–3 Generic Creative Communications Observation Form

Artist's Name: _____ **Class:** _____

School: _____

Brief description of activities observed:

Time 1:

Time 2:

Time 3:

Rating scale:
0 = not applicable; 1 = not evident (but should have been); 2 = poor;
3 = fair; 4 = good; 5 = excellent.
Please indicate the difference (+ or –) between the student at the beginning and end of residency. There is space for additional comments that might clarify the ratings and give a fuller sense of each student's growth and development.

#	Item: The teaching artist clearly *encourages* the following student behaviors:	1st Observation	2nd Observation	3rd Observation
1	Students exhibit concentration, focus.	0 1 2 3 4 5	0 1 2 3 4 5	0 1 2 3 4 5
2	Students communicate personal ideas verbally/visually.	0 1 2 3 4 5	0 1 2 3 4 5	0 1 2 3 4 5
3	Students use problem-solving skills.	0 1 2 3 4 5	0 1 2 3 4 5	0 1 2 3 4 5
4	Students create a mood or atmosphere in writing/art work.	0 1 2 3 4 5	0 1 2 3 4 5	0 1 2 3 4 5
5	Students create well-defined characters/images.	0 1 2 3 4 5	0 1 2 3 4 5	0 1 2 3 4 5
6	Students demonstrate control of new communication techniques.	0 1 2 3 4 5	0 1 2 3 4 5	0 1 2 3 4 5
7	Students follow directions regarding completing assignments.	0 1 2 3 4 5	0 1 2 3 4 5	0 1 2 3 4 5
8	Students demonstrate control of writing techniques such as metaphor, simile, and other poetry conventions.	0 1 2 3 4 5	0 1 2 3 4 5	0 1 2 3 4 5

continues

Figure 8–3   continued

#	Item: The teaching artist clearly *encourages* the following student behaviors:	1st Observation	2nd Observation	3rd Observation
9	Students demonstrate control of technical aspects of writing (spelling, grammar, punctuation, usage).	0 1 2 3 4 5	0 1 2 3 4 5	0 1 2 3 4 5
10	Students stick with a project to its conclusion.	0 1 2 3 4 5	0 1 2 3 4 5	0 1 2 3 4 5
11	Students accept constructive criticism from peers & instructor.	0 1 2 3 4 5	0 1 2 3 4 5	0 1 2 3 4 5
12	Students collaborate, work together.	0 1 2 3 4 5	0 1 2 3 4 5	0 1 2 3 4 5
13	Students reflect on their own work and edit/revise accordingly.	0 1 2 3 4 5	0 1 2 3 4 5	0 1 2 3 4 5
Total points				
Comments:				

Figure 8–4   Resident Artist Questionnaire

In order to assess progress made toward project goals and to plan for the future, would you please fill out the following questionnaire and return it to _____ by _____ . The information that you provide will help to inform the planning process for next year. Thank you.

Carol Fineberg, project evaluation consultant

Your name: _____   **Date:** _____

School assigned: _____   **Class(es):** _____

1. What were the most important concepts that you tried to teach your students? (Attach a copy of your lesson plans.)

2. Do you believe that *most* students developed an understanding of these concepts? If so, give examples that substantiate your claim. If not, please discuss your reasoning.

3. What skills did you try to teach the children? Do you think that most students acquired new skills or at least improved existing skills? Explain.

4. Were you able to identify particularly talented students? If so, please list their names and the characteristics that struck you about these children. (Use the back of this form if you need more space.)

5. Using the following scale—poor, fair, good, excellent—please rate your experience with the various aspects that support an artist residency. Use the space provided (or additional paper) to comment on any of these aspects (commendations, recommendations, etc.). Leave blank those items that were irrelevant to your residency.

Rating of Project Elements

Aspect of Residency / Comments	Poor	Fair	Good	Excellent
Planning				
Facilities				
Equipment				
Materials				
Student effort				
Teacher involvement				

6. What changes would you like to see incorporated into next year's program?

Figure 8–5   Professional Development Workshop Questionnaire

FORM   A   B   (Circle one) To be answered prior to enrollment in workshop and two or more months after participation in workshop.

The purpose of this questionnaire is to determine how the professional development workshops have influenced classroom practice. Would you please respond to the items below and give the completed form to _____ by _____. Thank you.

Dr. Carol Fineberg, project evaluation consultant

Today's date _____

Your name (optional) and school _____

1. Please list below the names of the workshop/institutes(s) you attended:

   A. _____

   B. _____

   C. _____

2. To what extent do you think the workshops influenced your teaching practices? Please circle the appropriate choice:

   A. To a great extent   B. To some extent

   C. To no appreciable extent

   If the answer to Item 2 was A or B, please describe what aspects of the workshops influenced your teaching practices by checking the appropriate choices below:

   ___ Used new teaching resources (texts, photos, curriculum units, videos, etc.)

   ___ Used arts as a way to reinforce problem solving or critical thinking

   ___ Used arts to reinforce historical and/or geographical understanding

   ___ Used arts to reinforce literacy skills

   ___ Used arts to reinforce math concepts or skills

   ___ Used arts to reinforce science concepts

   ___ Other (please describe) _____

3. (To be answered 2–3 months later) How would you describe the results of your trying out one or more of the arts related ideas you checked above?

4. What future workshops would serve your teaching purposes? Describe in the space provided.

Several texts are available that describe how to construct questionnaires, surveys, and other feedback instruments. One that I have found useful is *How to Conduct Surveys* by Kosecoff and Fink. I have also found it helpful to periodically review the essentials of performance or authentic assessment with my clients. The following checklist (Figure 8–6) has proved helpful.

Figure 8–6   The Essentials of Performance (and/or Authentic) Assessment

1. Determine purpose of assessment.
2. Identify and articulate clear standards against which to measure performance.
3. Develop appropriate tasks that will help measure:
   - performance
   - portfolio contents
   - demonstration of knowledge, research skills, higher-level thinking skills
   - exhibition quality
   - slide show/lecture/PowerPoint presentation
   - other special project
4. Establish criteria for assessing the successful completion of tasks using various instruments to measure performance:
   - rubrics (with interpretation of each point on the scale)
   - templates (to determine content)
   - checklists
5. Ensure reliable and valid scoring; ensure interrater reliability.
6. Enlist experts when necessary to validate or in other ways assist in the assessment process.
7. Analyze and report findings.

Program evaluation and assessment of student progress will always be with us. The challenge before arts organizations and educators concerned with the continuation of arts programming in the schools is to ensure that the process of measuring impact does not get in the way of the process itself. Teachers and teaching artists need not change the way they do things because "the evaluator is coming." On the other hand, we would expect that if during the process of evaluation, we find that the targets are being missed, then program planners should be amenable to examining the data and creating a process for problem solving.

I have always enjoyed the role of evaluator, primarily because my clients have genuinely wanted to know what I concluded from my observations. I have enjoyed the process of problem solving and have been gratified by the way programs have smoothly evolved after rather bumpy starts. The fact that most funders demand evaluations is a good thing; without this mandate, arts organizations, much less schools, would not pay as close attention to the results of what they are doing, and they would be weaker for it. There is a prevailing feeling that evaluations take good money out of the coffers that could be better spent in delivering services. Yet evaluations do not have to be expensive, nor do they necessarily have to be conducted by outsiders. In the final analysis, it is the data that counts, and in many instances the data can be collected by program staff. Program participants can reflect on the meaning of the data together and can make the kinds of changes needed to increase the power of their programs by themselves. But they have to collect good data, and they have to understand its implications. Many arts organizations find it more cost effective to engage an evaluation consultant than to try to add more tasks to the workload of already overburdened staff.

Assessment and High-Stakes Testing

Schools and arts organizations need to be warned that tying the arts to high-stakes reading and math tests might well result in uncertain if downright absent confirmation. How well I remember my crossed fingers when we did exactly that in an Arts Partners study and in the evaluation of Thinking Through the Arts. In each case, an analysis of the reading scores and scores on the Ross Test proved statistically significant. We could prove the value of the arts as an academic booster. But what if there were not such a correlation? We agree with Hedland and Winner that it is a dangerous game when the arts are hung on the peg of academic achievement. Although they may in many cases contribute to progress, in some cases they may not. Does that mean they are not valuable? If they do not result in academic achievement, then what? Do we dump them as being superfluous to the national plans for education? Of course not. Our children need the arts just as much as they need the humanities and sciences. At the same time, we want to ensure that arts programs are qualitatively on target and aligned with those characteristics and conditions that researchers have linked with success in various circumstances. And for this we need the rigorous practice of evaluation and assessment.

Identifying Conditions That Contribute to Exemplary Work 9

W hat are the conditions that contribute to excellence and enable the arts to thrive in schools? While evaluating scores of school-based arts in education programs over the past twenty years, I have been able to perceive a pattern of policy positions and behavior that seem to give some answers. The pattern coincides with what has been noted by several national research efforts, such as *Schools, Communities and the Arts* (1995), *Gaining the Arts Advantage* (1999), *Champions of Change* (1999), and *Critical Links* (2002).

The conditions are, as with many aspects of education, easy to label but difficult to accomplish. This chapter attempts to discuss some of these conditions and show that when the arts and education intersect, when the conditions are in place, good education and good art can be practiced. Conversely, when the most important conditions are missing, so is evidence that the arts are making a difference in learning. Good arts programs do not create the conditions for them to flourish. To think otherwise invites deep disappointment and an overestimation of what the arts can do in a given educational environment.

An effective school must have effective administrators, praiseworthy staff, a rigorous and animating curriculum, clear-eyed assessment and evaluation processes, and supervisory support for all players to do their best work, regardless of whether there is a good arts program. Good arts programs, if they are to serve a school's needs, require *visionary and enabling leadership, sufficient time for planning and implementation of good ideas,* and *artistic and pedagogic expertise* if they are to become viable supports for school reform.

The arts by themselves cannot transform a poor or mediocre school into an exemplary one. By forging a rhetorical marriage between the arts and school reform, the arts risk being blamed for school failure when, in fact, they are usually the victims of failing schools. If the conditions for excellence are in place, however, then all other aspects of school reform can be enhanced by the arts. Moreover, despite a poorly run school, an arts program may prosper as its own little island of excellence surrounded by a sea of mediocrity.

Leadership at the School Site

When we look at successful schools (i.e., that is schools with a safe and supportive climate, high or rising test scores, low staff turnover, articulated parent and community support, and outside validation of their teaching practices and learning outcomes), we usually find certain policies in place that support the best kind of education programs. One of the most frequently mentioned factors is, of course, leadership, with the understanding that leaders—the go-to people, the enablers of progress, the people who articulate powerfully on behalf of a constituency, the ones in the front of the line by acclamation as opposed to size—come in many guises and serve at various levels of school reform and governance. But the truly great leaders operate with a vision of what their schools can be, and they work hard to share this vision with their colleagues and parents.

Some education leaders have initiated arts programs that have demonstrated over time how the arts can help schools achieve certain school reform goals. Others have used their leadership virtues to help elevate the quality of existing arts programs and have expanded opportunities for children and youth to learn through the arts by finding resources to do so. Many of the strong administrators of recognized partnerships are in the foreground because of their leadership skills, which they have chosen to use in support of the arts. Strong and effective leaders have enabled colleagues to get together and examine their work as *critical friends,* a useful phrase introduced by the Coalition of Essential Schools. Other leaders give a platform to advocates for strong arts programs so their voices can be heard by school boards and the general community in which the school is located. Some leaders are visionary and leave the day-to-day implementation to others. Some leaders are heads of schools; others are faculty members or parents who provide the fuel for advocacy efforts as well as the technical know-how for programming.

Leaders of successful arts-centered schools take their students beyond the ordinary curriculum mandates, understanding that great schools must have strong programs that foster creativity and grow talent. They understand that through good arts programs, students can explore the key questions that civilizations must consider as they prepare their young to take on productive roles in society. We find that good schools (i.e., Blue Ribbon schools, schools cited by national studies, schools hailed in their own communities) are inevitably led by strong, intelligent, and skilled principals who help staff and parents formulate a consensus around clear and appropriate learning goals. Few schools succeed on multiple measures *despite* poor leadership at the top, and even fewer schools do well if district managers fail to cultivate strong leadership from within the faculty and parent body.

School leaders find that the arts can be a powerful aid to improving the learning environment. The arts can liberate teachers to find more creative ways to show the world to their young charges. They can be used, as has been mentioned in previous chapters, to heighten understanding of certain scientific principles, of mathematical structures, and of the power of technology to represent virtual reality. Although the arts cannot turn mediocre principals into extraordinary instructional leaders, they can help arm newly appointed principals and relatively benign administrators with strategies that will assist the revitalization of curriculum and instruction.

Several urban areas have developed Leadership Academies to grow a new generation of education leaders as principals and other key administrators retire. Some, like in New York City, address the needs associated with change and improvement by developing tracks for three unique groups:

- Aspiring principals.
- Principals who are new to the system (newly promoted and externally recruited).
- Incumbent principals.

Common to each of these programs is the emphasis on developing true instructional leaders. New York defines such leaders as those who "have strong vision and values that orient all school activities around student learning and academic growth. They create a sense of urgency and excitement about teaching and learning" [*www.nycleadershipacademy.org*].

Inexperienced principals who are eager to learn can find the arts useful in improving school morale by providing support for outstanding performances by professional artists, uplifting professional development by creating arts-infused experiences for them to learn from, and consistently including the arts in the yearly comprehensive educational plans. They can enlist professional artists (i.e., teachers, teaching artists, artists found in their own community) to work with students to design attractive spaces for learning. They can highlight best practices in their school for others to admire and possibly emulate. We have witnessed many transformations of relatively inexperienced principals into good and effective leaders as a result of their involvement in various arts-related professional development experiences.

By engaging with artists in various kinds of workshops, principals have found new techniques to relate to staff more effectively. They have also accepted artists' conviction that by giving youngsters useful formats within which to express what is on their minds, language skills will be improved.

There are too many cases of mediocre and fearful principals who block the arts as viable instructional components because they claim their students will not test well if they are taken off the prep-for-tests regimen. This has been disputed by many research studies (as listed in the Works Cited and Recommended Reading section), but sadly, poor leaders do not take risks and are more secure when they insist that teachers limit their work to test prep exercises and dreary reading texts than when pursuing good instructional practice.

Promise and Disappointments of Professional Development

Central to most efforts to improve schools is a professional development plan that combines training workshops and courses to fill in knowledge or skill gaps in members of the teaching staff. Outstanding principals use professional development budgets to help transform a critical mass of teachers from arts-absent to arts-present instructors. They enable teachers to learn how to plan and team effectively with artists, to acquire skill in arts-related active learning projects, and to build enthusiasm for what is essentially a more demanding pedagogy. Many school districts offer inservice credit and salary incentives to teachers who participate in professional development courses after school. Some districts will actually underwrite the cost of tuition for an advanced degree. More and more partnerships are developing between local universities and the nearby school districts to provide specifically tailored courses that enhance the school's arts education programs and also give participants opportunities to gain salary credit. St John's University in Queens, New York, is leading the way with seminars led by Anne Fritz on ways and means to integrate the arts into classrooms.

Professional development may be aimed at principals, other supervisors of instruction and curriculum, and/or teachers. In practice, professional development can be anything from a mass class in how to deal with a new directive (preventing child abuse or understanding how to fill out the new report card) to a workshop for a handful of teachers that gives them a fresh approach to an established curriculum.

The usual reason for professional development is to train principals and teachers to use a newly sanctioned curriculum (e.g., new or old math, phonics or whole language methods and materials) or procedures for dealing with a critical problem (e.g., child abuse, drugs, conflict). Rarely is a distinction made between training teachers or principals to do something and educating these same people in an area that escaped them when they were in college or graduate school.

As with everything else in education, certain conditions need to be present for any training effort for teachers and other school-based staff to result in positive attitudes and changes in practice. These conditions include the following:

- Clear understanding of what different groups of teachers need to be trained to do and segmenting training opportunities and requirements accordingly.
- An atmosphere where the professional development process is valued and supported between and after training sessions.
- Confidence among teachers and principals that the professional development will be worth their time.
- Expertise in both the content and process of training.
- Relevance to the tasks of teaching and learning.
- Willingness to ascertain that the planned training will have visible consequences in the classroom.

When it comes to educating principals and teachers in areas that were skipped or forgotten in formal preservice classes, the conditions are similar but with some additions:

- Opportunities for further education should be encouraged by management.
- Information regarding educational advancement should be regularly and openly disseminated.
- Those who learn new content should have an opportunity to share what they have learned with colleagues in an appropriate forum.
- Teachers and principals should be able to demonstrate what they have learned in real time and before interested observers.

Rarely are all conditions in place in one school building. The principal or her or his designate may not find the time to visit classes regularly to ensure that the training has "taken." Time constraints may limit training to a percentage of the time required. Trainers may be deficient in the required expertise. Insufficient time may be allocated to follow and get feedback on new practices, and a general lethargy regarding professional development may pervade the school, often reflecting reluctant building leadership.

The arts have provided an interesting prism through which to look at professional development thanks to state and local requirements that artists provide some sort of activity for teachers (and sometimes principals) in order to fulfill their obligations to agencies that fund them. Too often I see that the professional development opportunities in the arts are separate from the professional development opportunities built into schools' formal strategic plans for the year. This is unfortunate, because the arts could be called on to enhance teachers' abilities to deliver a more rigorous and stimulating instructional sequence in any subject.

Many artists offer an art-making session as part of their professional development commitment. For example, dancers might offer a dance class; painters might offer a class in painting or constructing an object along the lines of what they will be asking students to make; and musicians might offer a class in musical improvisation using the children's Orff instruments. These classes are generally fun, and the more enthusiastic (and skilled) teachers might use the session as a source of ideas for classroom follow-through. These sessions, usually voluntary, have little promise of reforming teacher practice, however. Rarely does anyone in the supervisory structure invest in the sessions as part of the school's improvement plan. They are nice departures from the usual workshops, but they have little impact on those who attend them.

I was surprised to discover when evaluating recipients of Ann-enberg grants for partnerships with arts organizations how few principals factored in arts programming as part of their mandated Comprehensive Education Plans. Nor was I heartened to discover that the arts as tools for learning are not included in any depth as part of the training for would-be principals in the various preappointment programs in most large cities.

One of the most successful professional development efforts—if success is based on enthusiastic response and evidence of classroom follow-through—was a weekly Arts Caravan inservice course that I facilitated for the New Rochelle schools. This course was so much in demand that we ran it every spring for several years while the district leadership was developing its comprehensive arts education plan. The course was an effort to familiarize teachers in both elementary and secondary schools with some of the cultural and aesthetic trends that were evident in the arts and cultural institutions of metropolitan New York, including Westchester County as well as New York City. We hired a bus to accommodate everyone who had registered and we visited avant garde installations at the Neuberger Museum and other local art galleries; we attended some off-off-Broadway plays on diffi-cult subjects (we saw the young actor, John Turturro, in one of his first professional appearances) and went to hear new work at the Metro-politan Opera and New York Philharmonic several times. We also attended some new dance ensembles performing locally and in New York City. After each event, we had a seminar in which we discussed our experiences and explored ways in which what we had attended could or did have some relevance to their lives as teachers. Everyone was required to write a paper at the end of the course reflecting on that same question. The course was particularly useful in moving teachers to a different understanding of what contemporary artists were about. And it was fun! We mixed culture with food, often eating together before or after the activity. We built a cadre of arts supporters within each school who, in turn, became the catalysts for further arts education activities in their schools.

I recently observed a consultant in dance education—who was also a coordinator of arts in education for a local school district—lead about fifteen elementary grade teachers through the English Lan-guage Arts standards. She then had them choreograph movement using skills analogous to the compositional skills needed to pass the English Language Arts state test. Sounds simple, but only a person with command of both dance and English composition could have pulled it off successfully. The teachers left the workshop feeling refreshed, but I was skeptical regarding whether any of them would try out the analogy in class. Unfortunately, I was right. Why? Because there was no support to do so once they returned to school. The professional development opportunity, sponsored by an exquisite dance company, was isolated from the school's power structure and did not result in any follow-through at the school.

The attempt to bring artists into the school to work with teachers requires a different tack on training. School-based personnel and resident artists need to work well with each other, but they are rarely given the time to develop a mode of operation that will result in smooth teamwork. Here is where professional development could have a dual payoff for both the practitioners of arts-integrated programs and the students themselves. Too often artists work as soloists in the classroom and need help in developing collaborative skills that will engage their alleged partners—the teachers—in the learning process. Similarly, teachers generally work as solo conductors of classroom activities and need help in planning and facilitating activities led by a resident artist. This kind of training, which cannot help but enhance the teaching skills of both artists and teachers, is rarely provided because of lack of time and money. Although some districts and arts organizations occasionally run professional development courses that try to encourage collaborative planning, they cannot substitute for on-site training that is designed to encourage immediate results in the behavior of trainees.

When professional development disappoints, it is usually because there is a lack of reflection on how workshop strategies can be incorporated by participants into their day-to-day work. Teaching artists given sporadic workshops without follow-up observations by either critical friends or staff from sponsoring arts organizations cannot be expected to adopt new ideas and formats after just a two-hour exposure to them. They need help, just as teachers do who are trained to use an art form with which they were unfamiliar before their workshop experience. Supervisors need to be part of professional development workshops so that they will know what to look for when they help teachers adopt new methods and materials. Although all of this is obvious, it is not often practiced in the field. Lack of time is the usual reason that professional development is such a fragmented enterprise. The skillful leader tries to weave professional development opportunities into a larger scheme, where it can be made accountable to school goals and objectives.

Networking as a Professional Development Strategy

From the time I worked with the New York City Board of Education on the Arts in General Education (AGE) program, I learned to value the power of networking to help people adopt new and improved professional behaviors. We worked a network of thirty-two separate schools into a confederation of principals who advocated for strong comprehensive arts in education schools. They visited each other's schools, eager to demonstrate one or more programs that reflected their view of arts in education. Some of the more experienced principals informally mentored some of their less experienced colleagues. Many developed personal friendships that lasted long after AGE had aged out!

Although networking enables a peer support group to help when trouble is brewing, or when there is an opportunity to collaborate on a funded program, there are weaknesses that need to be noted. One weakness of some networking strategies is a disinclination to think critically about programs in progress. There is such a need to put a positive public face on educational practice that it takes an extraordinary leader to admit that some efforts do not pan out, that some residencies are less than good, that some arts-infused programming is below par. In the early days of my work in the field, candid responses to mediocre work, especially that provided by outsiders, was rare and uttered only in the most confidential circumstances. As the field has matured, however, I see more criticism and greater efforts to ensure that the right relationship between provider of service and school is developed. I see schools becoming more demanding in their requirements. Principals or their agents are less reticent about turning away an arts organization if they feel that the work does not fit with the needs of the school. And they make an effort to see the provider's work as opposed to just responding when someone complains. It has pleased me as a grant maker to see schools weigh the advantages of one provider over another as they consider what services they need to provide through partnerships and what they need to offer as in-house continuous programs.

When I was asked to design an education program for Tony Randall's National Actors Theatre (NAT), we created a network of high school English teachers who taught drama as part of their job description. These teachers met with Tony and other members of the company before the opening of every new production. They previewed each new production prior to bringing their students to special morning performances scheduled for them. In their meetings with NAT artists, they explored different themes to work with their students before attending performances. Teachers and their classes saw plays by Ibsen, Arthur Miller, Gogol, and Chekhov during the first two seasons. As members of the audience, they responded with close attention to crucial and difficult passages in each play without getting restless. They had acted out these challenging scenes in class with professional actors dispatched by Young Audiences of New York, who worked in tandem with NAT. Because their teachers could prepare them well, and because the artists supplemented teachers' efforts by adding a professional artist's point of view, these students directly benefited from their teachers' professional development. As a result, the actors from NAT actually looked forward to student matinees as the high points in the subscription series. This network of teachers is still the core of the NAT education program, which is augmented by opportunities for other classes to purchase discount tickets through the box office.

A professional development strategy that continues to thrive today involves networking principals into group support teams where the arts become a theme that binds them together. It is always rewarding to see how experienced, arts-savvy principals encourage and teach their younger colleagues how to harness arts resources and use them to improve the educational programs in their schools. The less experienced find strength in the fact that arts-rich schools are likely to test well as long as the curriculum and instructional practices schoolwide are rigorous and linked to the logic behind testing instruments. They find they can have their arts and good testing scores too! Networks of principals were introduced to New York City public schools in 2003–2004 with the reorganization of the system by the Mayor and his Chancellor.

I was privileged to work with networks of principals in New York City, New Rochelle, and at Southern Westchester's Board of Cooperative Education Services (BOCES). In each case, principals learned well from each other and used their knowledge and skills to enhance their schools with outstanding arts programming. They hired full time instructors as soon as it was financially feasible; they contracted with arts organizations to augment the number of arts studios available to students; and they advanced learning through the arts by hiring artists/arts organizations to team with classroom teachers in creating experimental units of instruction. They passed around ideas for best practices and provided moral support for each other as needed.

Time to Do Things Well and Right

Principals are having a very tough time protecting their arts programming because of limitations on time mandated by the No Child Left Behind version of federal support for education and various state and local education department policies. They and their teachers feel terribly constrained by the high-stakes testing mandates and misunderstanding of the place of testing in the process of accountability. Many arts-rich schools are losing their gusto as a result of intimidated principals whose own performances will be judged primarily by student performance on standardized tests given once during the school year. Too much time is appropriated for read-and-drill exercises and not enough time is available for the arts in its many guises. The school day is at least an hour too short each day. Some schools offer funded after-school programs that incorporate arts programs, but they do not serve enough children or youth to make up for programs that should be part of the regular school day. As part of a regular, albeit extended, school day, the courses and teachers have the same footing as other subjects. After-school programs are inevitably marginalized.

In my study of the arts and cognition, it was very clear that schools acknowledged as excellent enabled teachers to plan and assess their work in teams on a regular basis. This was especially true when the planning sessions were facilitated by a coach or supervisor who could keep the group focused and productive. When these planning groups were then asked to include experts in the arts in their planning process, they were able to address the quality of arts-infused instructional programs in a timely fashion.

Time is a factor in creative work that is rarely addressed. Too often in both elementary and secondary school, insufficient time precludes the completion of quality creative work. Put another way, the creative process is squeezed into a time slot that makes it almost impossible to generate creative solutions of quality.

I was reminded of this problem recently when an artist and I discussed an impending assignment for him. The school wanted a playwright who would work with four classes once a week for ten forty to forty-five-minute sessions. Within that period of time, students in each class would be led through a playwriting process that would culminate in a production in the school's auditorium acted by, of course, the students in the class! Although the request may seem outrageous, it is typical of many that are negotiated between arts organizations and schools. In this instance, the playwright would help kids generate scenes, probably from improvisations, that would then be typed up and cast by the playwright for two or three hurried rehearsals culminating in a lifeless and unsatisfying production. For this effort, students would be expected to understand how plays are written and produced.

School representatives and artists who negotiate these programs need to remember that they are the controllers of quality in this educational venture. They need to use the rules of reason when they schedule activities and should try to be true to a genuine creative process that fits the time allotted. That usually means trimming expected outcomes to something less than the original idea. Instead of creating an auditorium production in 450 minutes, the school and artist might consider approaching playwriting from a totally different point of entry. What could be accomplished well in 450 minutes with support between sessions? How could the residency reach a conclusion with students, teacher, and artist satisfied with the results? The negotiation and planning processes should yield creative solutions that can be managed within given time constraints and, if they can't, frankly someone has to pull the plug. Students only learn negative lessons when they are forced through a poorly planned, inappropriate so-called creative exercise. And the arts lose a lot of potential advocates.

Expertise

An essential condition for successful arts programming is expertise. Because of the opportunities educators have to partner with arts organizations to create arts-integrated instruction, no one person has to be expert in both the arts and education. Artistic or pedagogic expertise is acquired over time and with an aggregation of good experience. In an ideal world, artists should be, first of all, good artists, recognized by their peers with appropriate artistic credits to their names. Teachers should be effective classroom instructors who know how to plan a thematic unit of instruction with appropriate goals, objectives, and anticipated outcomes that can be evaluated and/or assessed at the completion of the unit. Teachers should be able to manage their classes with a firm hand so that the artists can do their best work. Artists should be able to communicate well with their students, able to demonstrate what they mean by modeling the desired process or product. Sometimes the ideal road is hard to get to: not all teachers are expert, and not all artists are at the top of their field. School leaders have to ask themselves where the experts are in their buildings and how to best use them in providing instruction in and through the arts. They have to assess whether there is potential for expertise given opportunities for professional development and the time to practice new and improved skills. They certainly can be fussy about the incorporation of resident artists into their programs. And they can be careful about what performances and exhibitions are invited into the school so that children are not exposed to patronizing presentations that would not pass muster in any other venue.

Schools must become expert in detecting artistic quality. Sometimes committees of parents and teachers screen programs to see whether they are good enough for their schools. Sometimes they develop checklists that might look something like the one in Figure 9–1.

Figure 9–1 Observation Checklist: Potential Assembly Programs (Elementary and Middle Schools)

Item for a Music Program	Yes/No	Comments
1. Is it pleasant to hear the ensemble play?		Discuss repertoire, quality of performance
2. Do the ensemble players inform the audience of special features of the repertoire to listen for?		Melodies? Rhythms? Patterns? Historical placement? Style?
3. Do the ensemble players project good performance values?		Energy, concentration, audience awareness
4. Do you recommend this group to perform in your school?		Which grades?
5. Will there be an opportunity for children to interact with the artists?		How? Will the interaction be meaningful?
6. Other aspects of the program		

A similar observation checklist could be prepared for a theatrical presentation or a dance recital.

When Expertise Is Rare, What Then?

It is one thing when schools are located in arts-rich environments that attract the best and the brightest performers and visual artists.

New York, Los Angeles, and Chicago are obvious centers that attract not only the stars of tomorrow but also the stars of today. What if you live in a small rural area that is too far from a big city to be able to call on experienced, professional artists? What if your area is so isolated that the chances of first-class artists coming through town seem to be next to none. Happily, policy makers on the state and national level have been addressing this situation for some time. The NEA has launched several initiatives that send young, highly accomplished artists into the rural parts of the country to perform, exhibit, and conduct workshops for families and school groups. I had the extraordinary pleasure of seeing one of these efforts in full bloom when I was asked to evaluate an NEA-sponsored regrant program in Nebraska. The Guthrie Theatre from Minneapolis had mounted a wonderful production of *Great Expectations* and was able to tour the production to rural sites in the Midwest with additional support from the Mid America Arts Alliance. I visited Grand Forks, Nebraska, in time to see yellow school buses from a dozen different rural school districts arrive at the local high school, full of parents and their children, eager to see a live performance by one of the great repertory theaters of America. Their response to the performance was over the top—a ten-minute standing ovation! I also had a chance to chat with high schoolers who were helping the tech staff set up the scenery for the one-night performance. They were exhilarated by the experience, and some disclosed their ambitions to go to Lincoln and Omaha for college training in the arts. I also visited Salina, Kansas, where an exhibition of contemporary artists from the Midwest was installed at the local center for the arts. Again, rural populations attended in large numbers. At each instance, the sponsors successfully engaged school groups as audience and participation in exploratory workshops.

Efforts to reach underserved populations continue with the newly announced "NEH on the Road" traveling exhibitions and the well-received "Shakespeare in American Communities" project that is entering its third year. These projects carry on the tradition of making art of the highest caliber accessible to populations located far from traditional cultural centers. The NEA's efforts complement the efforts of each state arts agency. They make efforts to enable rural and other underserved areas of their states to access artist in schools programs under various headings. These programs help reduce the cultural isolation of outlying areas and help reduce the costs of importing artists into their communities.

As school faculties strive to increase their expertise in infusing the arts into the wider curriculum, teachers and principals are taking greater advantage of professional development opportunities provided by state Alliances for Arts Education that, with support from the Kennedy Center and local funding sources, frequently sponsor summer arts in education institutes. Those interested in accessing such training need only check the website [*www.kennedy-center.org/education/kcaaen*] for specific information for each state. Teachers in need of upgrading their skills regarding various aspects of arts education and arts-integrated practices can always contact their state and local education department arts education program directors as well as their local arts councils, which often sponsor professional development activities by collaborating with artists and educators in the vicinity.

Maintaining the Reforms

There are a number of lists kept by various private and public agencies as well as publications that seek to identify the best schools in the country. Two agencies that do this are Great Schools [*www.greatschools.net*] and School Match [*www.schoolmatch.com*], whose findings are published by *Newsweek* annually. In addition, the Department of Education lists the results of its annual search for excellence—the Blue Ribbon Schools, the best schools in each state according to its criteria, which include[1]:

- Student focus and support.
- School organization and culture.
- Challenging standards and curriculum.
- Active teaching and learning.
- Professional community.
- Leadership and educational vitality.
- School, family, and community partnerships.

It is not surprising that the overwhelming majority of these schools have vital arts programs, nor is it surprising that many of the magnet schools for the arts appear frequently on these lists. Where the lists are compiled yearly, such as by School Match, one can see many arts-rich schools cited year after year.

How do the long-termers do it? The answer is relatively simple: they work hard at maintaining the conditions of excellence. They watchdog their schools and make sure that as some leaders retire or transfer out, others of equal caliber are hired in their places. They

---

[1] See *www.ed.gov/offices/OERI/BlueRibbonSchools.*

insist on program protections (time, expertise) through energetic advocacy at school board and community gatherings and tireless efforts to gain additional funds from public and private sources. Islands of excellence are frequently aided by their reputations: funders are more likely to continue to support success than risk failure. They keep up to date on national and state initiatives that would perpetuate key program elements. They network. They publish or collaborate with others to publish their story. They care about excellence, so they insist on planning programs that fit time and space constraints rather than try to fit the wrong foot into the proverbial glass slipper.

What does it take to ensure that the promises of arts enhanced learning are kept? Happily, the best research yields a useful checklist that confirms what common sense would argue:

- Strong, intelligent leadership at the top and amidst the faculty and parents.
- Skill in budgeting appropriately to support instructional goals.
- Know-how regarding how to add resources to the basic instructional budget.
- Vision regarding what an arts-centered school should look like, feel like, and what best practices really are.
- Clear and appropriate learning goals.
- Praiseworthy staff.
- Effective, supportive administrators and supervisors.
- Clear-eyed assessment and evaluation processes.
- A sensible strategy for converting teachers from arts-absent to arts-present instructors.

The list is short, but the tasks are difficult. Outstanding schools must periodically reinvent themselves; they are in a continuous cycle of self-examination, paying attention to new circumstances as they arise, and adjusting to new opportunities as they occur. It is an exhausting process and can only be maintained if the responsibility for maintenance is shared by all stakeholders.

Schools of Choice 10

S chools of choice, because of their departure from the
norm in their communities, have the potential to
evolve into islands of excellence. This chapter examines four kinds of choices: charter schools, magnet
schools, theme schools, and small secondary schools.

Charter Schools

Charter schools are independently managed, publicly supported, nonsectarian schools that are open to all students and
not subject to the control of a local school district. They may
not charge tuition, and they cannot impose discriminatory
admissions requirements. Charter schools must follow all
applicable local and federal health, safety, and financial
accounting and reporting regulations.

The concept of a charter school has been very appealing
to certain political groups as well as to parents who are dis-
satisfied with what the public school system offers in their
community. The first charter schools began to appear in the
early 1990s, and as states have passed their particular versions
of enabling legislation, the number of charter schools nears
three thousand nationwide at this writing. About 10 percent of

all charter schools claim strong arts programs and the number increases yearly.

Governance is in the hands of an independent board of directors, but charter schools are accountable to the state for the academic progress of their students. Plans for a charter school, including policies for governance, hiring of personnel, curriculum, assessment, and professional development, as well as building maintenance and financial accountability, must be approved by the chartering agency, usually the state education department, before schools can open for business. No one is assigned to a charter school; parents, students, teachers, and administrators actively select their students and teachers.

Like magnet schools (see following section), charter schools are eligible for federal support on a competitive basis in addition to what they receive as their fair per-pupil expenditure from their states. Some charter schools began as desegregation magnets, seeing the conversion as a way to protect their school's unique features as state and local policies regarding desegregation have weakened. For example, many magnets have consistently operated across district lines in order to attract a mixed population. As localities are no longer obliged by court orders to desegregate, some districts are voiding policies that allowed parents to cross district lines in order to enroll their children in magnet schools. Charter schools are given permission to open by the state, and it is not a problem to enroll youngsters from several school districts into one charter school.

Charter schools that specialize in the arts have a particularly challenging task in finding additional money to support the arts programming. It is expensive to create an appropriate performing space with lights and sound systems, a studio for painting and sculpture, appropriate supportive technology, and the like. The state allocation is rarely sufficient to the purpose of a fine and performing arts school.

Charter schools are so much a part of the educational alternatives landscape that there are now organizations that serve both existing and would-be charter schools. *How Community-Based Organizations Can Start Charter Schools* by Frank Martinelli (Annie E. Casey Foundation, 2001) is just one of many books written to help local organizations to unite with interested parents to create an alternative to the public schools in their community. This is of particular interest to arts organizations that want to start arts-centered schools after their successful experiences as partners with schools.

Running a charter school is very difficult; just because the hierarchical demands have been reduced does not guarantee a successful school. This is patently clear as charters come up for renewal, having experienced thorough performance evaluations. Arts-centered charters are particularly difficult to bring to fruition because the number of variables to control increases so dramatically once one adds the complex demands of performing and visual arts instruction.

I have been particularly interested in the transformation of the Duke Ellington High School of the Arts as it moves toward quasi-charter designation within the District of Columbia. Having transformed from a specialized school to a magnet school to a quasi-charter school, it is now in a partnership with the John F. Kennedy Center for the Arts and is slowly moving out from under the administrative regulations of the D.C. Public Schools because of its unique mission. Regardless of its status, it is still charged with providing a daily program of rigorous academic and arts instruction. Its partnership with the Kennedy Center has strengthened its aesthetic programming, and its new governance configuration promises to enable the school to meet the needs of a diverse population of talented young people.

A group seeking a charter must submit a performance contract to the authorized entity detailing the school's mission, program, goals, students served, methods of assessment, and ways to measure success. The length of time for which charters are granted varies, but most are granted for three to five years. At the end of the term, the entity granting the charter may renew the school's contract. Charter schools are accountable to their sponsor—usually a state or local school board—to produce positive academic results and adhere to the charter contract. The Center for Education Reform is an excellent place to start collecting information regarding charter schools [*www.centerforeducationreform.org*]. They are linked with all charter schools in all areas under the jurisdiction of the U.S. government. For the legal definition of a charter school in a particular state, consult that state's charter school law through the Center's State Profiles area. For those interested in forming an arts-centered charter school, *Planning an Arts Centered School* (Fineberg, 2002) contains an informative section on how to begin and complete the process.

The charter school movement has roots in several other reform ideas, from alternative schools to site-based management, magnet schools, public school choice, privatization, and community–parental empowerment. The term *charter school* may have originated in New England in the 1970s during that decade's search for more relevant, educationally viable schools for the children of the Baby Boomer generation. The idea was promulgated by Albert Shanker, former president of the American Federation of Teachers (AFT), who liked the idea and suggested that local boards could charter an entire school with union and teacher approval. In the late 1980s, Philadelphia started several schools-within-schools and called them *charters*.

In 1991, Minnesota became the first state to authorize charter schools. These schools were developed according to three basic values: opportunity, choice, and responsibility for results. California followed suit in 1992. By 1995, nineteen states had signed laws allowing for the creation of charter schools, and by 2003 that number increased to forty states, Puerto Rico, and the District of Columbia. Charter schools are one of the fastest growing innovations in education policy, but they are not without their critics. Some are concerned about the standard of education offered by these free-floating islands, which are no longer able to count on the support of the local school district.

In his 1997 State of the Union Address, former President Clinton called for the creation of three thousand charter schools by the year 2002, and by 2003 his goal was within reach. In 2002, President Bush called for $200 million to support charter schools. His proposed budget called for another $100 million for a new Credit Enhancement for Charter Schools Facilities Program. Since 1994, the U.S. Department of Education has provided grants to support states' charter school efforts, starting with $6 million in fiscal year 1995. The list of charters is experiencing some major adjustments as schools that could not make the grade come up for charter renewal. While new schools are granted charters, others are having theirs rescinded because of a lack of evidence of educational success.

Magnet Schools

Most magnet schools of choice began as voluntary attempts to redress minority group isolation as a result of either *de facto* or *de jure* segregation practices before *Brown* v. *Board of Education* (1954). These schools have received or currently receive supplemental funds from state or federal governments to hire additional teachers, support an expanded curriculum, provide professional development of teachers and other ancillary personnel, and in many cases expand the number of class hours in a day beyond their school districts' norms. A few magnets were formed to attract students across school district lines, and some (without federal or state support) were created without any association with desegregation objectives but because a district wanted a thematic school.

Most magnets are either whole schools or "schools within schools" that focus on one or more innovative practices or themes. Magnets may focus on a particular aspect of the curriculum (e.g., communication, the arts, science and math, technology) and offer students more opportunities to study within that curriculum theme. Magnets may focus on a teaching method such as the Montessori method, or on a special program such as the International Baccalaureate or the Reggio Emilia early childhood model. There are hundreds of magnet schools located in the fifty states and Department of Defense schools; an exact number is not available because not all schools submit their data to the National Center for Educational Statistics. The Magnet Schools Association, a not-for-profit service organization, keeps track of funding sources and trends for its membership, which includes a sizeable proportion of existing magnet schools.

I first became acquainted with magnet schools shortly after the first legislation was passed enabling their creation. In 1978, I was invited to develop magnet schools for Teaneck, New Jersey, because of my reputation as an arts in education specialist. The school board had an idea that creating magnet schools could bring several million much-needed dollars into the district. Lynne Janicker, funded programs director, initiated a proposal development process that resulted in first a planning grant and then a multiyear implementation grant from the Department of Education that focused on the development and maintenance of arts-centered programs within each of Teaneck's schools: one at the high school, one at one of the two middle schools, and one at each of six elementary schools. Before the institution of the magnets, the arts were important to the residents of Teaneck, but they were not very important in the schools. Art and music were taught in the elementary and middle schools, and dance was taught at one of the middle schools. The high school offered the usual programs in art and music, and drama and dance were basically extracurricular. My job as a consultant to Teaneck's school system was to help a committee of parents, teachers, and students plan with the administration a detailed network of magnets that would attract students from families that were hitherto disengaged from the public schools and to encourage parents to continue to send their children to the middle and high schools where there was a serious decline in registration.

At this point in my career, I had just left the New York City school system, where I was Project Manager of the Arts in General Education (AGE) program, on a leave of absence in order to complete my doctoral studies at NYU. My reputation as a proposal writer was growing, and I was considered an authority on arts education as a result of my work with AGE. I had good people skills and was able to facilitate collaborative planning and engage various stakeholders in a process of consensus building regarding the purposes of a school. (I was also a trained mediator, having earned a certificate in Mediation and Conflict Resolution from Cornell.) Lynne knew that I could identify good arts programs in the area and could recommend adjunct artists of quality to work with Teaneck's elementary and secondary school students.

I had presented my programs at various conferences and had begun to publish articles about my work revolving around the arts in education. I wanted to examine the new phenomenon of artists working in schools, and I was also interested in putting my newly developed ideas about evaluation and assessment into practice. So when Lynne called me, I jumped at the chance to participate. My partner in C. F. Associates, Charlie Wilson, and I spent the next three years working with Teaneck's administrators, teachers, parents, and adjunct artists to craft a highly successful arts magnet program. Many of the original elements are still in place at this writing, and as with all things, the original magnet concept of the Arts Magnet has been reincarnated at the high school as the Teaneck Arts Academy, now in its second year.

Later in my career, after several years of working with New Rochelle, I was able to convince the superintendent and his staff that New Rochelle would be an excellent site for magnet schools. With a succession of assistant superintendents of elementary schools, I developed magnet school plans and wrote proposals for three of its elementary schools (Webster School of Arts and Humanities; Barnard Early Childhood Center, based on the Reggio Emilia model; and Columbus School of Science and Mathematics and Technology). Each of these schools continues to function as a magnet where students interested in enrolling are selected by lottery.

Magnet schools are differentiated from charter schools by their relationship to the local educational agency (LEA), usually a school district. They are not freed from the usual regulations, but work within the policies and rules that govern the whole district.

Magnet schools were introduced as a voluntary form of desegregation in the early 1970s; by 1978, the federal government was allocating millions of dollars to support magnets where either the local school district was under a court order to desegregate its schools or a pattern of de facto segregation, northern style, was enforcing a pattern of minority isolation. Of all methods of establishing, maintaining, or increasing racial balance and interracial harmony, magnets have proven to be one of the most popular. At this writing, magnet schools of the arts account for at least 25 percent of the funded magnet schools in the United States.

Theme Schools

A third category of schools that exist on the elementary and secondary level are those that are self-designated theme schools. With whatever discretionary money they can find, these schools provide an especially rich curriculum, and frequently the theme revolves around an arts-rich curriculum. They hire full-time teachers of art, music, dance, and drama and incorporate arts organizations into their instructional program to the extent that they can stretch their budget, including generous contributions from parents' associations. They are diligent regarding the way they spend their arts money. They hire full-time arts teachers who provide a stable core of arts experts. They augment this staff with long-term relationships with trusted arts organizations. Principals are actively engaged in overseeing their instructional programs, and they enlist faculty leaders to provide peer coaching.

Because of the many national and state organizations that identify exemplary educational practices, hundreds of designated model schools are cited yearly for their outstanding features. Arts Education Partnership, Americans for the Arts, the Kennedy Center, and the President's Committee for the Arts and Humanities are just a few of the national organizations that cite schools with exemplary programs. Model schools are usually those that have been recognized for their outstanding programs and the progress made by their students. They may be models of professional development, models for research, models of innovative curricula, or models of interdisciplinary study. Some are models of solutions regarding classroom discipline, the dropout rate, the achievement gap between minority and majority students, or models of English language acquisition. But beware: while a particular partnership may work well, this does not mean that the whole school's instructional program is a model of instructional virtue. And from year to year, schools can undergo major changes that alter the quality of their work.

Small High Schools

The past five years have seen a rise in what is called the small schools movement. The Bill and Melinda Gates Foundation has been particularly generous in providing funds to big cities where small schools seem to be providing a much-needed alternative to the large, impersonal, and troubled high schools. Working through existing regranting organizations, the Gates Foundation has made a huge investment in creating and sustaining small high schools with a particular set of standards based on their distillation of research on successful schools:

- *Common focus.* Staff and students are driven by a shared understanding of what an educated person is and what good teaching and learning look like. Every decision and every action is guided by this common vision.
- *High expectations.* Teachers are dedicated to helping students meet state and local standards. All students leave school prepared for success in college, work, and civic life.
- *Personalization.* The school promotes sustained relationships between students and adults; every student has an adult advocate.
- *Climate of respect and responsibility.* The environment is authoritative, safe, ethical, and studious; teachers model, teach, and expect responsible behavior; relationships are based on mutual respect.
- *Time to collaborate.* Teachers have time to work collaboratively with one another to meet the needs of all students: the school partners with businesses, civic organizations, and institutions of higher education to give students the best opportunities.
- *Performance-based.* Students are promoted to the next instructional level only when they have achieved competency. They receive extra help when they need it.
- *Technology as a tool.* Appropriate technologies are used to design learning opportunities and communicate with the public about performance.

Built into these standards are countless opportunities for the arts to serve the needs and interests of high schoolers, and it is no surprise that in New York, Kansas City, Los Angeles, Seattle, and Washington, D.C.—to name a few recipients of Gates grants—many of the small schools are planning rich arts and arts-integrated programming. Many of the existing New Visions Schools in New York City are arts centered with strong partnerships with theatre, dance, and music ensembles, museums, or arts organizations that specialize in placing professional artists in schools. The alliance between Epic Theatre Company and Talent Unlimited High School in Manhattan and Morris High School in the Bronx highlights the extraordinary impact professional actors and theatre technicians can have on the lives of rambunctious teens.

Whether the schools are charters, magnets, arts-centered traditional schools, or small high schools, it is clear that there are opportunities for the arts to assist in the creation of compelling models of education. The challenge to educational reformers, regardless of school configurations, remains the same: all of the instructional elements must be rigorous and demanding and include interaction with the canons of a multicultural legacy. There is no guarantee that a catalog of college prep classes will result in an island of excellence any more than will a catalog of arts offerings. Students must be taught well with good materials and stimulating teachers and world-widening experiences. And someday, our islands of excellence might form archipelagos! And archipelagos might join together to provide critical masses of excellence and a multiplicity of good choices for our nation's children and youth.

11 *Forecasting and Molding the Future*

*I*t is still very early in the twenty-first century to make predictions about the fate of public education one hundred years from now much less ten years from now. At this writing, the presidential election of 2004 is just months away. The campaign is full of rhetoric about education reform, although with the omnipresent foreign policy crises splashed across the front page, it is almost a luxury for the political adversaries to talk about education. A reading of *Education Week* suggests that the following issues are the focus of national attention:

Accountability
Achievement Gap
After-School Programs
Alternative Teacher
  Certification
Assessment
Character Education
Charter Schools
Choice
Class Size
College Access
Comprehensive School
  Reform

Desegregation
Distance Learning
Dropouts
English-Language Learners
High School Reform
Home Schooling
Low-Performing Schools
No Child Left Behind
Parent Involvement
Prekindergarten
Privatization of Public
  Education
Professional Development

Reading	Social Promotion
Religion in Schools	Special Education
School Construction	Standards
School Finance	Student Health
School-Based Management	Student Mobility
School-to-Work	Teacher Quality

Predictably, most of the issues fall into the obvious categories of curriculum, instruction, staffing, assessment, and accountability. Others relate specifically to money issues, and a few directly address issues of equity (e.g., racial, economic, gender, special needs).

The problem with forecasting the future is that the issues of today may all be displaced by some unforeseen, overarching issue of tomorrow. Certainly the issue of security will receive increasing attention for the foreseeable future as school boards are haunted by Columbine, Oklahoma City, and 9/11. The issues surrounding schools of choice will continue to be both political and educational fodder for pundits and planners alike. As more studies pop up regarding the utility of vouchers, one can safely predict that voucher proponents, especially those who want aid to nonpublic schools, will keep trying to promote this policy despite increasing evidence of their ineffectiveness in impacting low-achieving students (for whom vouchers were supposed to be especially helpful). The question of funding from national, state, and local governments will persist, particularly regarding issues of equity. The manner by which different states handle the problem of rich and poor school districts requires some imaginative thinking to break the tax-loathing logjam of naïve citizens who think that government does nothing but suck money from the working middle class. New generations of future taxpayers need to be educated regarding the notion of supporting the public good.

Education as we know it will probably bumble along in urban centers, moving from one great experiment to another. But we will be guilty as a society if we cannot find ways to provide a viable economic role for those who consistently score in the lowest quartile on standardized tests.

The Future of Arts Education

Much of the future of the arts in education will rely on how soon boards of education will establish longer mandated school days. Extending the school day and year, growth of the partnership process, alternative certification programs for teachers of nontraditional subjects (e.g., media and dance), and revision of the accountability movement could work very well for education in and through the arts. Clearly, the present pattern of industrial-age school schedules continues to work against the serious study of the arts and creative work in general. Modifications in the preparation of teachers for the twenty-first century that call for schools and departments of education in institutions of higher education to mandate preparation for teaching youngsters about their cultural heritages will require new courses and research projects. The growing influence of technology will affect not only instruction, but also the whole area of keeping track of student and teacher progress. In many secondary schools, laptop and handheld computers will undoubtedly be ubiquitous, often with the aid of federal grants. We can only hope that students learn precomputer skills before they are so tied to the sole use of computers for problem solving, research, and calculation.

As for the content of art, music, dance, drama, and the literary and media arts, something's got to give. Pedagogy has to change so more opportunities are available to address important ideas through an artistic medium. The dominant practice of art making needs to be augmented by art thinking that includes not only the usual Getty-style four horsemen of production, criticism, aesthetics, and history, but also provides room for invention and design. Increased time in studios will help to address the make-it-quick forty-five–minute art project or the dreary music lesson where kids learn to sing songs from reproduced pages of popular song lyrics. Technique needs to be taught in a context of expression. Hopefully, more teachers of music will turn to *good* software for composing original music that is both aesthetically and cognitively within their students' grasp. Cultural histories have to be told through examination of a variety of canons and not just the Euro-American definitions of what art is. There are many excellent teachers whose work points the way toward these changes, but their work needs to expand to all parts of the country. And all good work requires more time to do it, hence the need for extended days and school years.

More time should be spent planning for a future that is going to be different from the time in which we currently live. Of particular interest will be Microsoft's effort in Philadelphia to develop a School of the Future within the financial boundaries of that beleaguered city's education budget. Those who wish to follow the process can consult the website created for that purpose: *www.microsoft.com/education/ ?ID=SchoolofFuture*.

I look forward to seeing a model School of the Future that includes a curriculum that grapples with the unknown—how to forecast it, prepare for it, and develop prototypes of responses to schools that appear to be increasing their dependence on technology as the primary educational tool.

One of the strengths of good arts education is the nourishment of the imagination. That said, arts educators and teaching artists need to be included in local efforts at future forecasting.

Easy Forecasts

Despite the lack of a crystal ball, it seems safe to predict the persistence of certain trends in education, including *more small middle and high schools* thanks to the generosity of the Melissa and Bill Gates Foundation. It also seems likely that *partnerships will continue to flourish* between arts organizations and schools as the likelihood of schools being able to deliver a thorough and effective arts education without the help of resident artists and the use of cultural resources is both unlikely and undesirable. The organizations that were created in previous decades to propel educational reform will continue, for the most part, to foster experimentation in various aspects of learning, and their models will be emulated, more or less, as media attention focuses on them. We should be able to look forward to *the continued influence of certain centers of research* such as Harvard's Project Zero; Brown's Coalition of Essential Schools; the ATLAS Communities in Cambridge, Massachusetts; New American Schools in Alexandria, Virginia; and New Visions Schools in New York City, among others as they support, advise, and disseminate information about reform efforts.

We can also look forward to *continued emphasis on assessment based on test scores*, but with some humanizing modifications. We should also see a *declining influence on alternative assessment techniques* unless practitioners are able to meet criticisms of their practices.

We should be seeing *more arts-centered schools* judging by the current trend to create schools of choice around the arts. We should also see *the deconstruction of various systemic reform efforts* as cities, in particular, change superintendents every few years. Because few systemic reforms are sustained for more than the span of a superintendency, and without sustaining leadership, the funds for reorganization usually melt away quickly.

Extending the School Day and Year

Pleas for a longer school year are getting more attention, so it is fair to forecast that *the efforts to create schools with longer hours will continue to multiply*. Some efforts will be underwritten by federal competitive funds such as the 21st Century, schools of choice grants, and the Magnet Schools Assistance Program that enable schools to provide longer days. The continued *proliferation of charter schools* may also result in *schools with longer days and years*.

Experiments with longer days have already revealed certain problems and prospects:

- Late scheduled classes become flabby because of exhausted teachers and students.
- Content of late classes tends to be "remedial" or "artsy."
- Not everyone takes late classes, and those who do are the least enfranchised in the school.
- Teachers assigned to late classes may be the most junior staff members.
- The tyranny of bussing makes it difficult to have follow-up sessions with students after class.

Strategies to improve prospects for vital extended-day programs include the following:

- Create greater flexibility in late classes regarding content and tools of instruction.
- Make facilities for action learning more available (rehearsal space, auditorium, labs, studios, computers, etc.) for late classes.
- Create short-term, special-purpose classes (test prep) later in the day as well as project-based learning mini-courses.

The extended day will surely be a feature of more and more schools as the century evolves; there is just too much to learn to be accommodated in a six-hour day.

Growth in Number of School Partnerships with CBOs and Corporations

Research studies on partnerships are beginning to teach potential partners of the characteristics that make partnerships benefit students. Businesses as well as funders look positively on partnerships between schools and community-based organizations as well as commercial work venues. The Council for School Corporate Partnerships has issued some guidelines that promise to promote more and better partnerships. They suggest that partnerships should be based on shared values and philosophies and should adhere to the following principles:

- Begin with an open and frank discussion about values, goals, and needs.
- Respect and reflect the culture and goals of both the education and business partners.
- Support the core mission of the school.
- Bolster the academic, social, and physical well-being of students.
- Complement the social values and goals of the school, business partner, and the community.
- Clearly define short- and long-range goals.
- Focus on collaboration to determine activities that meet the goals of all involved.
- Be aligned with education goals and board policies of individual schools and/or districts.

A full description of guidelines and caveats may be found on their website [*www.corpschoolpartners.org*].

Corporate partnerships can strengthen arts education if schools emphasize the relationship between a strong arts background and the world of business and commerce. Some corporations are deeply invested in support of arts programs out of the personal conviction of the CEO. Those who turn to corporations need to do their research before applying for grants.

The future of arts education is cause for celebration by optimists and caution by skeptics. The optimists can celebrate because of the increasing attention arts education advocates have garnered for the cause. Skeptics need to be wary of advocates who promise too much virtue from the arts. They can periodically paint the arts into untenable situations, such as in the recent insinuation of the arts into high-stakes testing. Although the logic is sometimes compelling, the consequences can be as stultifying for the creative life as is a lack of opportunity. As advocacy continues, however, it is likely that protections for arts education will remain in place and even expand. But if advocacy lags, or becomes less effective, the arts will shrivel to their least demanding requirements. It is the national pattern, and it has not changed in fifty years.

Many arts-centered schools can show the way toward school reform. They organized into an effective dissemination network some thirty years ago as the International Network for Performing and Visual Arts Schools [*www.artsschoolsnetwork.org*]. Their annual conferences give planners and supporters of arts-centered schools a helpful forum to explore the arts and education, and they provide within their membership models of schools that have propitiated the two sides of a symbolic Janus: educational reform and quality instruction in and through the arts.

If there is such a thing as a penultimate word (the last word yet to be written), then it would be found in the phrase "advocate with excellence in mind." School reformers need to look to the arts to *assist* them to develop better schools. Arts advocates need school reformers in order to get and maintain a foothold on the dominant item on the national domestic agenda. Both groups need to marshal their arguments to policy makers carefully so that schools can continue to rise toward standards of excellence while nurturing the artistic seeds found in every child. At that point, the last word will be written.

Works Cited and Recommended Reading

Books

Allen, David, ed. 1998. *Assessing Student Learning: From Grading to Understanding.* New York: Teachers College Press.

Anderson, Lorin W. 1981. *Assessing Affective Characteristics in the Schools.* Boston: Allyn and Bacon, Inc.

Annenberg Institute for School Reform. 2003. *The Arts and School Reform: Lessons and Possibilities from the Annenberg Challenge Arts Projects.* Providence, RI: Author.

Beattie, Donna Kay. 1997. *Assessment in Art Education.* Worcester, MA: Davis Publications.

Bloom, Benjamin S., ed.1985. *Developing Talent in Young People.* New York: Ballantine Books.

Brookes, Mona. 1986. *Drawing with Children: A Creative Teaching and Learning Method that Works for Adults, Too.* Los Angeles: Jeremy P. Tarcher, Inc.

———. 1991. *Drawing for Older Children & Teens: A Creative Method for Adult Beginners, Too.* Los Angeles: Jeremy P. Tarcher, Inc.

California Arts Council. 2001. *Current Research in Arts Education: An Arts in Education Research Compendium.* Sacramento: Author.

Campbell, Linda, and Bruce Campbell. 1999. *Multiple Intelligences and Student Achievement: Success Stories from Six Schools.* Alexandria, VA: Association for Supervision and Curriculum Development.

Cannato, Vincent J. 2001. *The Ungovernable City: John Lindsay and His Struggle to Save New York.* New York: Basic Books.

Cohen, Elaine Pear, and Ruth Straus Gainer. 1995.*Art: Another Language for Learning*, 3rd ed. Portsmouth, NH: Heinemann.

Council for Basic Education. 1998. *Standards for Excellence in Education.* Washington, DC: Author. Distributed by Association for Supervision and Curriculum Development.

Deasy, Richard J., ed. 2002. *Critical Links: Learning in the Arts and Student Academic and Social Development.* Washington, DC: Arts Education Partnership.

Dewey, John and Evelyn Dewey. 1962. *Schools of Tomorrow.* New York: Dutton.

Dobbs, Stephen Mark. 1998. *Learning in and through Art: A Guide to Discipline-Based Art Education.* Los Angeles: J. Paul Getty Trust Publications.

———, ed. 1979. *Arts Education and Back to Basics.* Reston, VA: The National Art Education Association.

Dorn, Charles M., Stanley S. Madeja, and Frank R. Sabol. 2003. *Assessing Expressive Learning.* Mahwah, NJ: Lawrence Erlbaum Associates, Inc.

Edwards, Betty. 1979. *Drawing on the Right Side of the Brain.* Los Angeles: J.P. Tarcher, Inc.

Edwards, Carolyn, Lella Gandini, and George Forman, eds. 1993. *The Hundred Languages of Children: The Reggio Emilia Approach to Early Childhood Education.* Norwood, NJ: Ablex Publishing Corporation.

Eisner, Elliot W. 1997. *Educating Artistic Vision.* New York: Macmillan Publishing Company.

———. 1979. *The Educational Imagination: On the Design and Evaluation of School Programs.* New York: Macmillan Publishing Company.

———. 1991.*The Enlightened Eye: Qualitative Inquiry and the Enhancement of Educational Practice.* New York: Macmillan Publishing Company.

———. 1998. *The Kind of Schools We Need: Personal Essays.* Portsmouth, NH: Heinemann.

Ellis, Arthur K. and Carol J. Stuen. 1998. *The Interdisciplinary Curriculum.* Larchmont, New York: Eye on Education.

Fineberg, Carol Lynn. 1992. "The Arts and Cognition: A Study of the Relationship between Arts Partners Programs and the Development of Higher Level Thinking Processes in Elementary and Junior High School Students." Doctoral dissertation, New York University.

———, ed. 2003. *Planning an Arts-Centered School.* New York: Dana Press.

Finn, Chester E., Jr., and Herbert J. Walberg, ed. 1994. *Radical Education Reforms.* Berkeley, CA: McCutchan Publishing Corporation.

Fiske, Edward B, ed. 1999. *Champions of Change: The Impact of the Arts on Learning.* Washington, DC: Arts Education Partnership.

Gardner, Howard, and David Perkins, eds. 1988. *Art, Mind & Education: Research from Project Zoo.* Urbana: University of Illinois Press.

Glatthorn, Allan A. 1994. *Developing a Quality Curriculum.* Alexandria, VA: Association for Supervision and Curriculum Development.

Goleman, Daniel. 1995. *Emotional Intelligence: Why It Can Matter More Than IQ.* New York: Bantam Books.

Goodlad, John I. 1984. *A Place Called School: Prospects for the Future.* New York: McGraw-Hill.

Greene, Maxine. 1995. *Releasing the Imagination: Essays on Education, the Arts, and Social Change.* San Francisco: Jossey-Bass Inc.

Harland, John, Kay Kinder, Pippa Lord, et al. 2000. *Arts Education in Secondary Schools: Effects and Effectiveness.* Berkshire, England: National Foundation for Educational Research.

Harvard Educational Review. 1996. *Working Together Toward Reform.* Cambridge, MA: Author.

Herman, Joan L, Pamela R. Aschbacher, and Lynn Winters. 1992. *A Practical Guide to Alternative Assessment.* Alexandria, VA: Association for Supervision and Curriculum Development.

Hoffman, Nancy E., W. Michael Reed, and Gwen Socol Rosenbluth, eds. 1997. *Lessons from Restructuring Experiences: Stories of Change in Professional Development Schools.* Albany, New York: State University of New York Press.

Howe, Harold, II. 1993. *Thinking about Our Kids: An Agenda for American Education.* New York: The Free Press.

Jethabhal, Hasan M., ed. 1989. *Voices.* New Rochelle, NY: New Rochelle High School.

Korzenik, Diana. 1985. *Drawn to Art: A Nineteenth-Century American Dream.* Hanover: University Press of New England.

Kosecoff, Jacqueline and Arlene Fink. 1998. *How to Conduct Surveys.* Beverly Hills: Sage.

Kozol, Jonathon. 1991. *Savage Inequalities: Children in America's Schools.* New York: Crown Publishers, Inc.

Lageman, Ellen Condliffe, and Lee S. Shulman, eds. 1999. *Issues in Education Research: Problems and Possibilities.* San Francisco: Jossey-Bass.

Lambert, Linda. 1998. *Building Leadership Capacity in Schools.* Alexandria, VA: Association for Supervision and Curriculum Development.

———. 2003. *Leadership Capacity for Lasting School Improvement.* Alexandria, VA: Association for Supervision and Curriculum Development.

Lewin, Larry, and Betty Jean Shoemaker. 1998. *Great Performances: Creating Classroom-Based Assessment Tasks.* Alexandria: VA: Association for Supervision and Curriculum Development..

London, Peter. 1994. *Step Outside: Community-Based Art Education.* Portsmouth, NH: Heinemann.

Longley, Laura, ed. 1999. *Gaining the Arts Advantage: Lessons from School Districts that Value Arts Education.* Washington, DC: President's Committee on the Arts and the Humanities and Arts Education Partnership.

Lopate, Phillip, ed. 1979. *Journal of a Living Experiment.* New York: Teachers and Writers Collaborative.

Madeja, Stanley S., ed. 1978. *The Arts, Cognition, and Basic Skills.* St. Louis: CEMREL, Inc.

———. 1977. *Arts and Aesthetics: An Agenda for the Future.* St. Louis: CEMREL, Inc.

——— and Sheila Onuska, eds. 1977. *Through the Arts to the Aesthetic: The CEMREL Aesthetic Education Curriculum.* St. Louis: CEMREL, Inc.

Marzano, Robert J., Debra J. Pickering, and Jane E. Pollock. 2001. *Classroom Instruction that Works: Research-Based Strategies for Increasing Student Achievement.* Alexandria, VA: Association for Supervision and Curriculum Development.

———. 2000. *Transforming Classroom Grading.* Alexandria, VA: Association for Supervision and Curriculum Development.

National Association of Secondary School Principals. 1996. *Breaking Ranks: Changing An American Institution.* Reston, VA: Author.

Miller, Karen. 1985. *Ages and Stages: Developmental Descriptions & Activities; Birth through Eight Years.* Chelsea, MA: Telshare Publishing Co., Inc.

Patterson, Jerry L. 1993. *Leadership for Tomorrow's Schools.* Alexandria, VA: Association for Supervision and Curriculum Development.

Podair, Jerald E. 2002. *The Strike that Changed New York: Blacks, Whites, and the Ocean Hill–Brownsville Crisis.* New Haven: Yale University Press.

Remer, Jane. 1990. *Changing Schools through the Arts: How to Build on the Power of an Idea.* New York: ACA Books.

Rich, Barbara, Jane L. Polin, and Stephen J. Marcus. 2003. *Acts of Achievement: The Role of Performing Arts Centers in Education.* New York: Dana Press.

Rief, Linda and Maureen Barbieri, eds. 1995. *All that Matters: What Is It We Value in School and Beyond?* Portsmouth, NH: Heinemann.

Rockefeller, David, Jr., 1977. *Coming to Our Senses: The Significance of the Arts for American Education.* New York: McGraw-Hill Book Company.

Schmoker, Mike. 2001. *The Results FieldBook: Practical Strategies from Dramatically Improved Schools.* Alexandria, VA: Association for Supervision and Curriculum Development.

Sheive, Linda T., and Marian B. Schoenheit, eds. 1987. *Leadership: Examining the Elusive.* Alexandria, VA: Association for Supervision and Curriculum Development.

Waxman, Hersholt C., and Herbert J. Walberg, eds. 1991. *Effective Teaching: Current Research.* Berkley, CA: McCutchan Publishing Corporation.

Welch, Nancy, and Andrea Greene, eds. 1995. *Schools, Communities, and the Arts: A Research Compendium.* Washington, DC: National Endowment for the Arts.

Winner, Ellen. 1982. *Invented Worlds: The Psychology of the Arts.* Cambridge, MA: Harvard University Press.

Reports

Annenberg Institute for School Reform at Brown University. 2003. *The Arts and School Reform.* Providence, RI: Annenberg Foundation.

Pergouhi, Svajian, Carol Fineberg, and Andrea Zakin. 1991. *Look and Look Again: Children's Art from Armenia.* New York: Armenian General Benevolent Union.

ArtForum. 1995. *Celebration & Crisis: What Artists and Writers are Saying about the Arts and Creativity in American Schools.* (ArtForum, June 1995).

The Arts, Education, and Americans, Inc., 1980. "A Series of Reports from The Arts, Education, and Americans." *People and Places: Reaching Beyond the Schools.* 1, *Your School District and the Arts: A Self-Assessment.* 2, *Local School Boards and the Arts: A Call for Leadership.* 3, *Ideas and Money for Expanding School Arts Programs.* New York: Author.

Consortium of National Arts Education Associations. 1994. *National Standards for Arts Education.* Reston, VA: Music Educators National Conference.

Eisner, Elliot W. 1988.*The Role of Discipline-Based Art Education.* Los Angeles: The Getty Center for Education in the Arts.

The Getty Center for Education in the Arts. 1986 *Beyond Creating: Roundtable Series.* Los Angeles: Author.

The Getty Center for Education in the Arts. 1987. *Discipline-Based Art Education: What Forms Will It Take?* Los Angeles: Author.

The Getty Center for Education in the Arts, 1989. *Education in Art: Future Building.* Los Angeles: Author.

Levine, Mindy. 2002. *Powerful Voices: Developing High Impact Arts Programs for Teens.* New York: Surdna Foundation.

Literacy in the Arts Task Force. 1989. *An Imperative for New Jersey Schools. A Survey of Arts Organizations, A Survey of Schools.* Trenton, NJ: Alliance for Arts Education.

Music Educators National Conference, 1994. *The Vision for Arts Education in the 21st Century: The Ideas and Ideals behind the Development of the National Standards for Education in the Arts.* Reston, VA: Author.

National Endowment for the Arts, 1988. *Toward Civilization* Washington, DC: Author.

Journals

Aprill, Arnold. 2001. "Toward a Finer Description of the Connection between Arts Education and Student Achievement." *Arts Education Policy Review* 102: 25–26.

Chapman, Laura H. 2001. "Can the Arts Win Hearts and Minds?" *Arts Education Policy Review.* 102: 21–23.

Educational Leadership: New Needs, New Curriculum. December 2003–January 2004. 61, no. 4.

Fineberg, Carol Lynn. 1994. "Collaborations and the Conundrums They Breed: Introduction to the Symposium on Community Resources." *Arts Education Policy Review.* 95: 9–11.

Gee, Constance Bumgarner. 2001. "The Perils and Parables of Research on Research." *Arts Education Policy Review.* 102: 31–38.

Hagood, Thomas K. 2001. "Dance to Read or Dance to Dance?" *Arts Education Policy Review.* 102: 27–29.

Harvard Educational Review. Spring 1999. 69, no. 1.

Hetland, Lois, and Ellen Winner. 2001. "The Arts and Academic Achievement: What the Evidence Shows." *Arts Education Policy Review.* 102: 3–6.

Hope, Samuel. 2001. "REAP: More than Fifteen Minutes?" *Arts Education Policy Review.* 102: 7–9.

Smith, Ralph A. 2001. "The Harvard REAP Study: Inherent versus Instrumental Values" *Arts Education Policy Review.* 102: 11–14.

Teaching Artist Journal. 2003. 1, nos. 1–4.

The New England Conservatory Journal for Learning through Music. Summer 2003. 2nd issue.

Urice, John K. 2001. "Implications of the REAP Report on Advocacy." *Arts Education Policy Review* 102: 15–19.

Assessment Instruments

Bracken, Bruce A. 1992. *Multidimensional Self Concept Scale.* Austin, TX: Pro-ed, Inc. *www.proedinc.com.*

Bowman, Garda W., and Rochelle S. Mayer. 1974. *The Brace System of Interaction Analysis.* New York: Bank Street College of Education.

Index